VESSELS OF HONOR

What it takes to be used by God

By Raashid K Brown

Edited by Jan Werner

ROYSTON
Publishing

BK Royston Publishing
P. O. Box 4321
Jeffersonville, IN 47131
502-802-5385
http://www.bkroystonpublishing.com
bkroystonpublishing@gmail.com

© Copyright – 2017

All Rights Reserved. No part of this book may be reproduced, stored in a retrieval system, or transmitted by any means without the written permission of the author.

Cover Design: Brahma Bull Marketing | brahmabullmarketing.com
Cover Image © Shutterstock by Permission and Standard License

ISBN: 978-1-946111-40-1

Printed in the United States of America

DEDICATION

This book is dedicated to my family and friends who have supported and encouraged me through the years. Your private and public support is greatly appreciated. Much love to you all!

ACKNOWLEDGMENT

I'd first like to thank my Lord and Savior Jesus Christ for giving me the gifts, calling, and opportunities that He saw fit to allot me. Despite my shortcomings, failures and proclivities, He still chooses to use me. I'm humbled and grateful.

I'd like to thank my family & friends for consistently supporting me.

Lastly, I'd like to acknowledge a lady who has helped me discover and sharpen my voice in this season of my life. This beautiful woman was my high school English teacher and the editor of this book. Jan, thank you for truly being a Vessel of Honor! You are remarkable and a great example of a Godly woman. Thank you for consistently sowing seeds of greatness into "at risk" students for 20 years. Your seeds landed in good soil. More Grace!

Table of Contents

DEDICATIONS	iii
ACKNOWLEDGMENTS	v
INTRODUCTION	ix
VEHICLES OF HONOR	1
THE EXCHANGE	23
TREASURE IN EARTHEN VESSELS	43
PRESSURE ON VESSELS	61
NEW WINE IN OLD SKINS	75
AVAILABLE VESSELS	87
LOYALTY	103
VESSELS MUST BE EMPTY	117
VESSELS MUST BE DEVELOPED	139
VESSELS MUST HAVE PASSION	153
VESSELS MUST BE PURGED	169
A PERSONAL LETTER TO YOU!	187

Introduction

While I was writing my first book; *You are the Greatest Discovery,"* I received a revelation from God that birthed the book that you now hold. One morning I was watching the news, looking at the senseless and lawless acts that were going on around the world and in America. Several unarmed black men had been killed in the streets, our nation was being inundated with political propaganda and protests were popping up all over the nation. It seemed like our country was becoming more and more dysfunctional and delusional. In the 29 years of my life, I'd never seen our world in this condition.

While watching the news, God started speaking to me. I remember hearing His voice so clearly. He said, "It seems as though, in these moments and at this time, I'm not present." As He said that, my mind could hear and see people crying out in pain, frustration and anger, "Where is

God?" Mothers and fathers of victims killed in the street had tears streaming down their faces, communities were in an uproar, life was not being valued and chaos seemed to be everywhere. God said, "It's not that I'm not present. The issue is that I don't have any vessels that I can use." Instantly, I became stirred in my spirit for days.

What do you do when God says something like that? For days, I kept having visions of vessels impacting the world. God was telling me that He was in need of people He could work through. I know there are millions of Christians around the world. Although that may be true, how many of those millions are willing to be used of God right now? I can't answer that question. Can anyone?

Instead of spending time regurgitating the problem, trying to find blame and even beating myself up for missing an opportunity when I could have been used, I started writing. I understand now why God placed this burden in my spirit to write this book. Its purpose is to help those of us who desire to be used by God anywhere, at any time, for anything!

Some people mistakenly think that once they have received Christ into their life, there is nothing else that needs to be done. You have your ticket into heaven and now you can do whatever you like. This is oh so far from truth! Yes, it is very important that you receive Christ into your life! That's the only way to get into heaven, but there is also work for you to do while you occupy this space and time on earth. In order to be used of God; to His highest and best use, you need to become a vessel of honor.

There is a purpose for your existence. Yes, attending church and Bible study, reading your Bible and being a good person are great, but God also wants to use you to impact the world for His glory! God has already provided our salvation. He sent His Son to die for our sins! That was the ultimate gift He could give to us. Now, it's up to you and me to be available for His power and anointing to flow through us to effect change in our world. What does it take to be used of God? What is required to be used? These two questions will be answered in this book.

At the end of each chapter, you will find what I like to call, *Chapter Appraisals*. These appraisals are to: 1) assist you in retaining what you read in each chapter and 2) assist you in your prayer life. Each question is meant to help you go further in your personal time with God as you ask Him to help you become who it is He has created, called and purposed you to be. These questions were challenging for me. I hope they are for you, too.

I believe this book will confront, challenge and change you from the inside out. God has called you to do more and be more than what you are now. He wants to use you to His highest and best use. Become a Vessel of Honor!

VESSELS OF HONOR

Vessels of Honor

Chapter 1: Vessels of Honor

Without even thinking about it, we all use vessels every day. A water bottle, a toothpaste container, a coffee mug, a teapot—they all have one thing in common. They are vessels. Some are large while others are small. Vessels have become so indispensible that marketing companies spend millions of dollars to ensure that the right colors, right time length, best angles, and more are captured, challenging us to buy their products. Merriam Webster defines *vessel* as, "a container for holding something." It's so simple—anything that has the capacity to hold, carry or contain something is a vessel. A ship, a car, a cup, a building, a house-- vessels. It doesn't matter how big or small, how old or young, what color, what ethnicity, what background, how odd it looks or how different it is. All vessels don't look alike. They don't share the same qualities. In fact, they don't cost the same amount of money. Although there are many disparities among them, the only thing that qualifies them as a vessel is the ability to hold something. If a substance can occupy the inside of something, then what can be occupied becomes a vessel.

Now that we have a clear understanding of what a vessel is, let's take a look at how vessels are made. Vessels are made through a process. When we see clay, we may think that the process of becoming a vessel starts there; however, that is false. In fact, clay must go through a process, to ensure that it is usable for pottery. Clay that is found in the ground is not suitable for pottery initially. Clay has to endure a series of processes. Once clay has been found, it must first be excavated and allowed to weather for weeks. After weeks of weathering, the dry material is dumped into a

Vessels of Honor

trough and covered in sea water to soften the lumps. After the lumps are softened, they are stirred until all of the lumps have disintegrated into a slimy, muddy substance called slip. The slip is then drawn off and settles into a tank where the stones and lumps are removed. After the stones and lumps are removed, the clay is given time to settle. After settling, the clay must be treaded upon. Finally, after clay has been treaded, it must sit for a period of time; isolated, so that its pliability is given time to improve.

All of this has to take place before the vessel even gets on the potter's wheel. It's necessary! Without this process, the clay will be defective and will not have what it takes to be durable. Process! Without process, the clay would simply be mud. There's a big distinction between mud and clay. The distinction can be so subtle that it takes skilled artists to see the difference. Mud and clay can be all different colors, shapes and sizes. The main difference between the two is in how they respond when they are directly impacted by heat. Mud stiffens and becomes hard. Clay softens. As it is with clay and mud, so it is with people. If you want to see what type of vessel a person really is, pay attention to how they respond to heated situations. Mud hardens because it refuses to submit to the process that heat introduces. Clay submits to the process and develops into something suitable and usable. Although mud can be used, sturdy vessels are made of clay.

When we hear the word *'vessel,'* several things may come to mind. There is one vessel that you have overlooked though. This particular vessel is the only one of its kind and actually has the ability to harm and even destroy itself! This vessel

Vessels of Honor

carries greatness in the form of creative ideas, innovative thoughts and great intellectualism than can birth valuable ideas to bring solutions to the world's problems and plagues. This vessel was the only creation God spoke into existence. He touched and formed it with His own hand. This vessel is one that was created to make an impact on the world in amazing and extraordinary ways. After this vessel is removed from the Earth, people will still be talking about what this vessel carried. This vessel has been redeemed with the ultimate gift. This vessel is YOU!

There's a story recorded in the Bible that sheds light on what it means to be a vessel. Jeremiah 18 records that a young prophet; named Jeremiah, was instructed by God to take a trip to the potter's house to receive a message from God. When Jeremiah arrives at the potter's house, he observes the potter working with clay on the potter's wheel. Verse 4 says that the clay was marred in the hands of the potter. The word '*marred*,' in Hebrew means "to destroy or go to ruin."

    The Bible doesn't say how long the potter had been working with this piece, but pottery work is tedious. The potter has to be focused, concentrated and skilled to be effective. Pieces of clay and dust are everywhere. The potter gets messy while using the potter's wheel. None of that matters, as long as the vessel is forming and moving like the potter wants. Have you ever felt like your life went to ruin all of a sudden? Have you ever had everything mapped out, planned out and figured out, and then—all of a sudden—your plans go awry and fail? Imagine the frustration the potter must

Vessels of Honor

have felt in that moment when the clay was destroyed.

In that moment of frustration, the potter does something amazing. He doesn't throw away the destroyed piece. He doesn't even take it off the wheel. Jeremiah 18:1 (KJV) continues: "so he made it again another vessel, as seemed good to the potter to make it." The Message Bible says it this way: "the potter would simply start over and use the same clay to make another pot." Why? Because the potter has invested too much into the clay to simply throw it away. Remember, the clay had to go through a process to become useable. Throwing the clay away would mean the potter would lose out on the investment that he made. It's worth the effort for the potter to start over again with the marred clay.

Raashid K. Brown

If you have messed up, fallen short, didn't do everything correctly, made some mistakes, and even done some things intentionally that you later regretted, you still have a purpose! God, the Potter, wants to use you, the vessel. In fact, He didn't turn the clay into just anything. He turned the destroyed clay into another vessel. That's good news! Even with your mistakes, He still wants to use you. There's no reason for you to live in the shame of what you did. One of the biggest strategies of our adversary is to discourage you from becoming the vessel God intended you to be. Today is the day that you get up and get back on the wheel, so God can continue to work on you!

Metaphorically, both the potter and clay have responsibilities in the process of making the clay reusable. The first thing that must take place is the clay must fess-up. The clay must admit that it is not being formed into the intentions of the potter. The next thing that must happen is the clay must become willing to submit to the process of being reshaped into something else. Could it be that the frustration you are or have been or are currently experiencing is due to you refusing to submit to the process of becoming another vessel? You must submit to the process of change. Lastly, the potter has the responsibility to apply water to the clay so that it becomes formable and easy to shape. Clay cannot be molded without water. It's an essential element in the process. In the Bible, water is symbolic of grace (John 19:34) and the life--giving and regenerative power of the Holy Spirit (Ezekiel 47:1-12). In order to become the vessel that God intends for you to be, you need grace and the Holy Spirit.

There is something else in this story that I think will encourage you. The clay becomes destroyed and messed up while it is in the potter's hand and on the wheel. While it is yet being worked on, it comes to apparent ruin. Sometimes, in your walk with Christ, you are going to make mistakes. Although you have to live with the consequences of your mistakes, you don't have to live under condemnation. God knew what mistakes you would make and still chose you! You are still in the Potter's hands! If you are still in His hands, that means the Potter still has His hands on you! The Potter must have direct contact with the clay in order to shape it. Pottery work is dirty business, but the Potter knows just what He wants to make you into. Mistakes, shortcomings and downfalls; you are still His vessel.

Vessels of Honor

I once heard a story about two watering pots in an African village. These two watering pots sat at the gate and were available for community use. Anyone; at any time, could use either pot. Although there were two pots, there was only one that people would consistently use. The one that was of constant use in the village was new, colorful and had beautiful artistry on it. The other flower pot was old and cracked, due to years of constant use. People in the village would wait in line for hours to use the new watering pot. It seems that any time something is new, everyone is excited and will invest their money, time and energy into having the first access to it. Everyone did just that, except a little girl named Anna.

Anna loved the old watering pot. She preferred it over the new one. Every day, around noon, Anna would come to the gate of the village and grab the old watering pot. The line for the new watering pot would be long, but people would wait without even considering using the other pot. Anna would; confidently and cheerfully, walk past all the onlookers. Whistling a tune that she loved, she would grab the old cracked watering pot, fill it with water, and take the journey back to her tent. This continued for months. Eventually, people got used to Anna using the cracked pot. Nobody would notice when she came to get it.

One day, while making the journey back, the bold watering pot came alive while being carried by Anna. The old pot inquired, "Why do you use me every day? I'm cracked and I'm old! Everyone sees that I'm available, but nobody chooses me except you." Anna didn't respond immediately; she just continued to walk. About 100 yards down the path Anna said, "This is why I pick you." Much

Vessels of Honor

to the old pot's surprise, there was a long row of beautiful delicate roses that blossomed due to the water that leaked from the old pot! The cracked pot was finally able to see that it served a greater purpose after all.

You may be like the cracked pot. You may feel like you are damaged, overlooked and not useful. It may appear that others are getting used more than you; getting places quicker or moving faster than you. Although that may seem true, know that right where you are you still serve a purpose! Someone is still getting life from you. Even your mistakes, shortcomings, situations and circumstances are helping someone else out. I'd dare to say that you are indeed perfectly flawed! Those imperfections that you had were so that you could water someone else's dream by your cracks. Your cracks serve a purpose!

God knows who you are, and what you were going to be before the foundation of the world (Ephesians 1:4, Jeremiah 2:11). You need to know and understand that. God knew you. The original word that Apostle Paul wrote for foundation is *katabole,* which means sowing or depositing. It is a word that was used to describe the act of conception. Before your parents conceived you, you existed to God. He knew you! Why is that important today? Because everything that you have done or will do, was already factored in beforehand. God knew the good, the bad, the great and the weak things about you; beforehand, and still hand-picked you for a purpose and a plan!

You are a vessel created by God for a purpose. There's a reason why you are on the Earth right now. You have a purpose. You have the ability to hold, carry and maintain riches in the form of gifts, callings, creativity, intellectual thought and concepts, innovative ideas and power. These things can't be purchased. They already reside inside of you! They are waiting to be discovered and used. They are lying dormant, locked down inside of you. These things are waiting for you to find the key, so they can be released. God already did the hard part. That was creating you. The next things that need to happen are that you need to discover who you are, what is inside of you and become a useable vessel. The effectiveness and impact that we will have depends solely on us. God created you; but what kind of vessel you will be, is totally up to you.

While spiritual awareness seems to be rapidly decreasing there are other alarming things rising astronomically—murders, divorces, scandals, sex crimes, drug trades, political issues, social injustices, depression, suicide, substance abuse, sexual misconduct and etc. It seems like evil is winning everywhere. As a matter of fact, we have become people who are accustomed to living in the middle. We are comfortable living in between panic and peace, crisis and calmness. One minute, our emotions are stirred due to something negative taking place either in our lives or in our community. The next, we are celebrating an accomplishment with friends or doing something positive for someone else.

So many people are living on the residue of times past, rather than having a sincere, authentic and effective dose of something that is relevant today. We are rising into new leadership roles, while not having a real experience with a holy God. We have fallen in love with church and the emotional attributes of it, while missing the communion with our Maker and Creator. Issues

Vessels of Honor

that once were prevalent only in the world, now have crept into the body of Christ. Apostle Paul said to the church of Ephesians, "But fornication, and all uncleanness, or covetousness, let it not be once named among you, as becomes saints." (Ephesians 5:3 KJV). Slowly but surely, these things have started to become normal occurrences in the body of Christ today.

In an effort to be more "relevant" in a world that is perishing every day, we have allowed some of the world's ideologies and pathologies into the church and allowed people to function with scarcity of character and poor leadership. The Western church in America has focused more on programs, entertainment and catchy sermon titles to keep people rather than on building people up to become vessels of honor. These issues and more have allowed us to slowly become vessels not worthy enough (by default of character and authenticity) to hold, maintain and carry the anointing of the Lord and to be the servants that He has called us to be. Many great and mighty women and men of God; who were sages of their day, used their gifts and callings to effect change in the world. Once they departed Earth, their mantles have fallen to the ground because few vessels are in place to carry them.

Mantles are meant for us to use on Earth for the glory of God. Mantles are earthly ordinary things that produce heavenly results. Mantles are used to transmit the power of God. Mantles endue God's power into the lives of people who wear them. In Biblical times, a mantle was a garment worn as a covering. In the spiritual realm, mantles are still garments—they can't be seen but their manifestations are felt. They are like oxygen; you

Vessels of Honor

can't see it but you know if someone has it or not. The power is not in the garment. The power is in the anointing that is on the chosen vessel. What qualifies a person for a mantle? The type of vessel that they are qualifies them. Common vessels cannot have great mantles. They don't qualify!

Common vessels can't have great mantles because instead of the glory going back to God, they would take the glory unto themselves. Common vessels with great mantles would become self-centered and egotistical. They would spend valuable time comparing themselves to others rather than working effectively to win souls to Christ. There are mantles of anointing, authority, healing, business, deliverance, evangelism, pastoring, prayer, etc. that have yet to be activated in the Earth because there aren't enough vessels fit for the Master's use.

Everyone has the potential to carry a mantle. God had your purpose and impact in mind when He created you. Your mantle will give you favor and authority to advance the Kingdom of God. Mantles come with a cost; it will cost you something to carry the mantle God has for you. It doesn't and shouldn't come easy. You may have to suffer for the mantle. For some, the mantle will come out of the tears of your suffering and pain. Once you get your mantle, you must protect it at all costs. It becomes the covering over what is contained inside of you.

Vessels of Honor

Chapter Appraisal

1) As a vessel, describe the gifts, talents and callings that currently reside inside of you.

_____

_____

_____

_____

_____

_____

2) Where are you in the process of having the Potter shape you as a vessel?

_____

_____

_____

_____

3) What mantel(s) do you have on your life? What mantels do you desire to have? Remember, there are many different types of mantels.

God created you, but it's up to you to determine what type of vessel you will be!

Vessels of Honor

Chapter 2: The Exchange

2 Timothy is one of three books that is deemed a pastoral book of the Bible. In this book, Apostle Paul writes to give directions to Timothy, as well as to encourage him to have endurance, be strong in grace, and be steadfast in what he has been taught. Paul warns Timothy of days ahead in which apostasy and godlessness would come.

2 Timothy 2:20 (KJV) states, "But in a great house there are not only vessels of gold and of silver, but also of wood and of earth; and some to honour, and some to dishonour." The great house Paul was telling Timothy about was the Kingdom of God. Oh, what a great, magnificent and glorious house it is! For some, getting in the house is all that matters. Some are totally good with that. Once they get a seat in the Kingdom and are secure in the fact that if they were to die today they know that

Heaven would be their home, they are good. Wrong!

Getting in isn't good enough! That may go against your theology and your idea, but just securing your ticket to heaven is not enough. That would be equivalent to driving from your residence to a ballpark, paying for parking, standing in the long line to get in, finding your seat and then sitting in silence with your hands across your chest as you wait until the game is over. It's a waste. If you are going to do what it takes to get in the house, you may as well enjoy the ambience, the magnificence and the joy of it! As it is with that analogy, so it is with some who enter the Kingdom. They enter in and become complacent. That is not the will of God for your life. He wants to use you, not just have you in the Kingdom.

Vessels of Honor

He says that in this great house there are two types of vessels. The Message Bible says this about vessels: "There are not only crystal goblets and silver platters, but waste cans and compost buckets—some containers used to serve fine meals, others to take out the garbage" (2 Timothy 2:20). Here Paul states that there are two kinds of vessels. One kind serves with honor. The word honor in the Greek language is *time,* and means "price," or figuratively it means, "the value willingly assigned to something (Strong's Concordance 5092).

The value of a vessel is not determined by the vessel itself—no matter how nice it may look or how great it may be priced. The value of the vessel is determined by what is contained inside of it. What the vessel carries is what makes and determines its value. While some people get star-struck by vessels, one must remember the vessel isn't anything but mere clay. Clay is good, but it is not meant to be worshipped. It's what the vessel carries; or has the potential to carry, that makes it valuable.

The vessel is not to be worshipped; the vessel itself must have a sense of value. Before you and I knew who we would be, someone had already paid the price to buy you. There was a transaction that took place in which life and blood was exchanged for you. Someone knew that you were valuable, so the Person paid the ultimate price for you. The transaction was called redemption! The Bible records in Romans 5:8 (NIV), "But God demonstrated his own love for us in this: While we were still sinners Christ died."

While you were still waiting to be born; while you were still a twinkle in your father's eye before the foundations of the world. While you

Vessels of Honor

were living life and not even thinking about Him, Jesus Christ exclusively handpicked you. Not only did He pick us before we knew about Him, He performed the ultimate business transaction with us in mind. He died! His death was a business transaction. In business, we call transactions; exchanges. In the spiritual realm, God calls it redemption. He gave up His life so that He could buy you and use you as His vessel. Therefore, the vessel itself has value. It must be treated honorably, because it was not easy to come by. Vessels of honor are generally stored in different places than regular vessels. Vessels of honor are used for special occasions.

In my grandmother's house, she has a curio cabinet in her dining room. A curio cabinet is simply a glass cabinet with metal or wood framework, used to display collections or objects.

Raashid K. Brown

In the curio cabinet, there are platters, plates, glasses and bowls. This particular curio cabinet has been sitting in the same spot all of my life. It has contained the same items all of my life. I never got a change to ask her why she chose those particular items, and how much she paid for them. However; based on their being in that cabinet, they obviously meant something to her. She set these particular items apart for special use.

    My family has always gathered at my grandmother's house every major holiday for a time of fellowship, fun and lots of laughter. During those momentous times, my grandmother never once used any of the vessels in the curio cabinet for anything. We had family dinners where we had expensive meals, but she never went to the curio cabinet and got a vessel out for anyone of us to use. Although they were never used, they were never dusty. They

Vessels of Honor

always had a shine to them. She would clean them off and ensure that they stayed looking presentable, but they would be put back in place and left alone. They were put in a special place on display, set apart from the others.

The curio cabinet served as a protection for the vessels that my grandmother had inside. In order to get one of the vessels, there was a door on the front that opened. The door served a purpose; it was the only way you could get one of the vessels. You couldn't come from the side, and you definitely couldn't come from behind. You had to open up the door and go directly to what you wanted.

Like my grandma, God has honorable vessels that He has purposely set apart for special use. To be set apart for special use is defined as being sanctified. When some people hear the word 'sanctified,' the first thing that comes to mind is running, jumping, shouting and dancing in certain churches. Although that emotional response is attributed to some, the definition of sanctification means: to be set aside for special use. As a Vessel of Honor, God wants to ensure that you are set aside for a particular reason and for a special purpose. That purpose is to be His Vessel of Honor.

In law enforcement, there is a term that is seldom used; but when it is, it denotes something special and unique. This term is used only when something is valuable and needs to be secured for the sake of preserving it for a later use. As a law enforcement officer, I can only recount a few times that I have ever heard this term used. Each time it was relating to a major crime and/or investigation. The term that I'm speaking about is 'protective custody.'

Vessels of Honor

Protective custody is confinement or restriction of a person, place or thing for protection to prevent harm or death from either outside sources or other persons. The key to protective custody is that there is confinement and/or restriction for protection. In some cases, the person is taken to a special place or hidden in a certain area where others cannot go.

As a Vessel of Honor; you may not know this, but you have been in protective custody. God has hidden you, confined you and restricted you for a purpose! One of the reasons is that He hid you to ensure that you would still be intact when He wanted to use you. Now, that doesn't mean that you have been a perfect vessel who has not made mistakes, done some things wrong or failed in some areas. What that means is that; even in your shortcomings, He only allowed those things to come against you that would not break you or destroy you. Those things may have hurt you, may have caused you some scars and may have caused a great deal of adversity, but they couldn't take you out.

God has had you in protective custody, because the treasure that is inside of you is not ready to be revealed yet. Although what you have inside of you is great, the people meant to receive the treasure are not ready yet. They still must walk through some things and get to a place where they need to receive what you have to give. Your treasure is not just valuable to you; it is valuable to the world! There are some people whose ears are tuned to hear your voice alone. Their noses were created to smell the fragrance that emits from you when you do what you do. Their eyes were created to behold the treasure that lies inside of you. It's

Vessels of Honor

not until they are put in the right place; in the right time, that they will find you.

Although I could spend a lot more time talking about the vessels of honor, Paul doesn't just talk about honorable vessels. He goes on to say, "but (referring to vessels) also of wood and of earth." These vessels are called vessels of dishonor. The word 'dishonor' used here is *atima* in the Greek language and means 'perceived as without recognized value and/or common use' (Strong's Concordance 819). A vessel whose value isn't recognized, or that is common, is considered a dishonorable vessel.

There's something missing is the world. The world is looking for it and can't find it. There are problems in the world that could be solved by it, but it's nowhere to be found. There are people who are living their lives in hope that they stumble into it, but presently it is yet to be seen. Some things that we have become comfortable with will cease to exist, once we discover it. What's missing? Vessels of Honor!

So many people are doing great and wonderful things, but they aren't being used to their highest and best use. There are some who just simply meet the demand given to them, but they aren't going to the levels of excellence to which they've been destined. Vessels of Honor are individuals whom God can use, in places that would give Him the most glory. They will be most effective in the areas to which He has called them. These vessels are life changing. They are atmosphere changers. They set standards just by their mere presence.

So many wonder, "How is it that a human being can be a vessel?" While the thought may

Vessels of Honor

seem strange to some, the reality of the thought is true. Your employer uses you as a vessel. In your marriage, you are a vessel. In your community, you are a vessel. In every area of social, relational or economic influence you have, you are a vessel. You are being used to render help, service, training, assistance and many other services to different people at different times. Everybody is a vessel. Everyone is being used by something or someone. The question isn't, "Are you a vessel?" The question is, "What type of vessel are you?" Are you really a vessel of honor? The Bible states that you can be, but what do you say about yourself?

While reading an article about a well-known investor, I read a statement of his that I thought was amazing. In the article, the wealthy investor was sharing tips and concepts that allowed him to become wealthy. The investor said that no matter the circumstances or his enthusiasm to get involved, he disciplined himself to challenge himself to think about one thing; price vs. value. He explained his reasoning: Price is what you pay; value is what you get.

Having that concept in mind, I'd like to pose a question to you. How much do you cost? When someone wants to be a part of your life, when someone wants to use you, when someone wants you to be a part of their vision, goal or dream, how much do you cost? What is your brand? When you walk into a room, what comes into that room? When you are asked to respond, participate or partner with someone, what is the other person getting from you?

We would all like to think that we are priced at a good price. We would like to think we are expensive. The fact of the matter is, nobody should

Vessels of Honor

be able to determine your price but you. You set the price tag! Often, we allow others to determine how much we cost by allowing them to treat us how they feel, and not by what we are truly worth. Since you determine your own price; when it comes to being used by others, you determine how people handle you.

In 1967; near Mount Kilimanjaro, a tribesman found something that resembled a stone. The contrast of what he saw led him to believe that it was something far more precious than that. The stone was thought to be a sapphire. After a series of tests, it was determined that the sapphire-like crystal was; in fact, a blue violet crystal known as 'Tanzanite.' Tanzanite is ranked as the 2nd most popular colored gemstone in the United States. It has been said that Tanzanite is a thousand times rarer that diamonds. The mines in the Masai region;

where this stoned was found, are projected to run out of this particular crystal by 2030. Because of the rarity and the color, Tanzanite jewelry is expensive. The price of it was determined by how rare it is.

As it is for Tanzanite jewelry, so it is with you. You are a rare vessel—so rare that there will never be another you ever again! You broke the mold! You can be imitated, but you can never be duplicated. Since you are so valuable; so rare and so special, govern yourself like it. Don't let anyone else make you out to be less than who you are. Price should not be solely determined by what is seen. What also should come into play is what you get—value!

Value is one of the most important aspects of anything in life. In some cases, the value of something cannot be readily seen. Through a

Vessels of Honor

process of time, supply and demand and the authenticity of an object, the value of it will be determined. You have to know what it is that others should expect when they get you. It takes away a lot of the wondering that comes along with partnerships, relationships, friendships and etc., when you know what value you have to offer.

Again, price (what you pay) and value (what you get) are important. As it relates to vessels, one doesn't mind spending a large sum of money when that vessel will hold up to its value. One of the biggest disappointments is paying a price for something that doesn't live up to its value. Sometimes a vessel isn't living up to its value, because it is not being used correctly. If you are building a home, a hammer is valuable. If you try to take that same hammer and screw in a nail, it will not hold up to its value because you are not using it correctly. Screw drivers turn screws, hammers drive forging objects together.

  When it comes to being an effective vessel, a portion of your price is determined by the need of the person who is willing to pay. It's not that you are a bad person, you are worthless, you don't have what it takes or you are not the one destined to do great things. It could be that you are not the tool needed at the time for the job to be accomplished. Using a hammer to screw in a nail during construction may work one or two times, but you can't complete a job effectively by using a hammer in the wrong way. When it comes time to need a tool like you, God knows exactly where you are and He knows exactly who needs you. Trust Him and His timing to put you where you need to be, when you need to be there.

Vessels of Honor

Chapter Appraisal

1) What value have you placed on yourself?

_____

_____

_____

_____

_____

_____

_____

2) In what ways and in what areas have you noticed that you are set apart from others? What is different about you?

_____

_____

_____

_____

_____

_____

_____

3) As it relates to price vs. value, when someone decides to partner, join or connect with you, what are they getting? Who are you consistently?

_____

_____

_____

_____

_____

_____

_____

Vessels of Honor are individuals God can use at any time and are the most effective in the areas where He has called them.

Vessels of Honor

Chapter 3: Treasure in Earthen Vessels

You have a treasure inside of you! Right now; in this current moment and at this current time, there is a treasure inside of you. No one can take it out, destiny pirates cannot steal it, and the treasure will not lose its value. Deep down in the reservoir of your being; hidden within the mechanics of your body, is a treasure. Merriam Webster defines treasure as "something valuable (such as money, jewels, gold or silver) that is hidden or kept in a safe place." Hidden jewels are inside of you.

Often times when we think of a treasure, we think of money. The movies show that at the end of the rainbow, the end of the journey or the end of the road, there will be a treasure box found full of money. Although money is great to have, money is not what is inside of you. If someone were to cut you open, you would not bleed out money like at ATM machine. One scripture that I often hear quoted; especially when it comes to getting money for something, is a portion of Deuteronomy 8:18 (KJV): "But thou shalt remember the LORD thy God: for it is he that giveth thee power to get wealth." Although we know that He gives us the power, what does that really mean?

In Hebrew, the word that we use for power is *koach*. *Koach* means ability, power and strength. God has put ability, power and strength inside of you that will cause you to get wealth. What an investment! You have the ability to be innovative, creative and dynamic. You have power to be impactful and explosive, reaching far beyond your imagination. There is strength to carry, to maintain and to fulfill the vision that God has put inside of

Vessels of Honor

you. All of this is inside of you right now! This treasure was placed inside of you from the foundation of the world. He put something down inside of you that is second to none. He broke the mold when He made you! What He put inside of you in the form of ability, power and strength, will spring up like a river of living water once you discover and tap into it. Again, the ability, power and strength inside of you is not money. It's something far greater that. It is giftings, talents, thought, standards, innovative ideas, creativity, teachings, ministries, callings, dexterity, nations, people and generations. It's far beyond currency.

In his letter to the Corinthian church; Apostle Paul says, "But we have this treasure in earthen vessels, that the excellency of the power may be of God, and not of us" (2 Corinthians 4:7). Again, YOU have a treasure inside of you. When

Paul wrote the word treasure here, he had something far greater in mind. The word treasure in Greek is *thesaurus* (Strong's 2344), and it means "a storehouse for precious things." There is a storehouse inside of you! A storehouse is a building where large amounts of supplies are kept for future use. I once worked in a place where I would frequent a storehouse. The storehouse had pallets of varied inventory from cups to mechanical parts. When we needed a supply of something, we wouldn't have to call the company to get it made. We would simply go to the storehouse, because; prior to the season getting started, the managers would order large quantities to ensure that we had enough to last through the season.

As it was with my former job, so it is with you and me in the kingdom. God has placed riches; in the form of abilities, strengths and power, inside

Vessels of Honor

of you that are needed for the world. When someone cries out to God for a solution; for an answer or for something to be done to fix whatever problem may be at hand, God doesn't have to go back to the dirt and create a man all over again. No! He simply goes to His storehouse and places you; His Vessel of Honor, in the needed situation. What you have inside of you is what others need.

Courage is rarely talked about, but plays a huge part in you becoming the vessel that God created you to be. You must have courage within yourself to dare to be different. Courage to pull out the creative, dynamic and purposeful treasure that is inside of you -- Courage to stand in the midst of adversity and in the middle of chaos. Courage is the power that enables one to do something difficult and dangerous. For the treasure that is inside of you to be discovered and unleashed, you must have the courage to birth it through action. As the definition states, it will be difficult and dangerous. The odds may look like they are against you. It may feel like you do not have what it takes to make it happen. Let me encourage you, YOU DO! How do I know? --Because God would never have put something in you that you don't have the ability, power and strength to pull out.

Jealousy is not even worth entertaining or having. God has graced all of us in His storehouse to walk in certain areas and do certain things that only we can do. We; as His earthen vessels, didn't choose the areas that we are passionate about. No! The manager who is over the storehouse knew what He needed. He placed each of us in areas and in atmospheres that need the treasure that we have inside of us.

Vessels of Honor

Furthermore, I want to encourage those of you who may be in a place or places, where you are not comfortable. These places may be getting on your nerves, driving you crazy, and/or leaving you frustrated and upset much of the time. Chaos seems to be breaking out everywhere. Dysfunction seems to be all over. Sometimes; as vessels, we can become worn out by letting cares, dysfunction, frustration and chaos pull us away from places where we are meant to make the greatest impact. We must get liberated and delivered from the thought that says, 'If things aren't right, then that must mean we are not in the right place, area, church, organization, family, career field or etc.'

God seldom puts people in a place or a position that is perfect and without trouble or error. God gets glory when His vessels are in problematic positions and places. God doesn't get glory out of perfection. That's Who He is! He chooses to place His vessels in places that are out of order, where there is question of the outcome, where something is dirty, where it looks as if something is about to fall apart, where the bottom is about to fall out and where things look hopeless and are going down a spiraling path leading to destruction. Why? Because when the solution is manifested and things are working together for good, we will see that no one could have fixed the problems but God!

Your light (your treasure) was not meant to shine against others' light. That's competition. Your light (treasure) was meant to shine in areas of darkness. --The darker the area, the brighter the light. If light shines in the darkest of times, those who see the light will have a better appreciation of it. People shouldn't have to look hard or even wonder about your good works. If you are placed

Vessels of Honor

in a dark place, situation or circumstance, let your light (your treasure) shine so that ultimately God will get the glory. Matthew 5:16 says, "In the same way, let your light shine before others, that they may see your good works, and glorify your Father which is in heaven."

Even though it may not feel good, you have to stay committed to where you are and stay focused. He would not have placed you there if the treasure inside of you wasn't needed. Your treasure is necessary! It's a mystery that He would put His treasure in an earthen vessel. God made His earth vessel; Man, out of dust (Genesis 2:7). Who puts gold inside of dust? Dust has the ability to make the treasure look terrible. Imagine if someone gave you a gift, but it was covered in dust. What would you think about them? What would you say that person thinks about you? Only God invests His treasure into dust! Knowing that through choices, proclivities, dysfunctions and failures, we have the capability to degrade the treasure. He still chose to place it inside of you. What joy it is to know that God thinks so much of me that He was willing to put His treasure in something made from dust.

If God was willing to invest so much into you, then you shouldn't have a problem investing yourself into discovering the treasure inside of you. The truth is that it's not your treasure. If it were, then I could understand your being selfish about it. Sometimes when people discover something good, they tend to hold on to it so that they have an advantage others don't have. While it makes sense and it is easy to do, you can't afford to be selfish about the treasure that is inside of you. Someone else's destiny is attached to the treasure inside of you.

Vessels of Honor

The latter part of 2 Corinthians 4:7 tells us why it's not about us. It says, "…that the excellency of the power may be of God, and not of us." What did Paul mean when he wrote, 'excellency?' After all, he is talking about vessels. When Paul wrote the word 'excellency,' he wasn't talking about exceptional or magnificent status. Paul meant surpassing excellence, beyond measure and exceeding greatness.

When one pours, gives, serves or does anything from the treasure that is inside of them; something happens. Greatness; as it relates to your purpose and destiny, begins to become more apparent to you. But it doesn't stop at greatness. The treasure that is inside of you should cause you to exceed greatness! That's how powerful the treasure inside of you is. It should go beyond all limitations, all barriers, all greatness and all excellence! It is so magnificent that there is no reference point to which you can refer. There will be no one for you to call to make sure that you are on the right track and going at the right pace. When one surpasses excellence exceedingly and beyond measure, that is the power that only God can give. The power that you have been searching for, wondering and pondering about is inside of you! The power is related to the treasure. Once you find your treasure, the power will come.

The first thing that needs to happen is for you to discover the treasure that is inside of you. It may be covered by hurts, disappointments, mistakes, failures, rejections, short-comings, divorce, setbacks and excuses. It doesn't matter what is covering it, it is still a treasure. Earlier I talked about giving a gift covered in dust to someone. The joy of having a relationship with

Vessels of Honor

Jesus Christ and having Him as your Lord and Savior, is that He has a way of fixing those things that are dust-covered and allowing those things to work for you. Remember, all of that was factored in when He chose you. I know for myself, I wanted God to erase some things so that the memory would be deleted from my mind. What He assured me of was those things were needed to make me who I am! The things that you have been through—the storms that you have survived, the decisions that you have made—have all helped make you into the vessel He wants you to be. It was all necessary.

While we do acknowledge having these components that have helped us become the vessels that He needs us to be, we can't be broken vessels. He wants us to be whole. There is danger in being a broken vessel. Being a broken vessel is equivalent to being a broken glass. If a glass is broken, why would we serve something in that vessel? You could hurt yourself or swallow glass drinking from a broken glass. It's important that you know that in order for God to best use you, you need to be whole. Whole vessels have the capacity to maintain, hold and remain consistent to the integrity of what is poured inside of them. There's nothing worse than drinking from a glass that has a crack in it. So it is true with a broken vessel. YOU NEED TO BE WHOLE!

Jesus Christ came in the expressed image of God. He was God, but came in the form of a man. John 1:1 (KJV) says, "In the beginning was the Word, and the Word was with God, and the Word was God." Verse 14 in the same chapter says, "The Word became human and made his home among us. He was full of unfailing love and faithfulness. And we have seen his glory, the glory

Vessels of Honor

of the Father's one and only Son." The first 18 verses of the book of John tell us about God taking on human flesh. Jesus came, tapped into His treasure, fulfilled His purpose, reached His destiny and died. Keep in mind, He did all that within 33 years. Start to finish, He was done! He was God, He took the form of a human. His body was mutilated, stabbed, pierced and destroyed. Why do you need to know, understand and take solace in that? --Because God, Divinity, became a vessel, humanity. Hs body was beaten, tortured and ripped. He was mutilated for you! His vessel was broken, so ours could become whole!

God wants to heal you, save you and deliver you so you can have the highest and best use for Him. No cracks, no limits, no barriers and no leaks. He wants you whole. Ninety-nine and a half will not do.

Chapter Appraisal

1) What treasure(s) have you discovered in yourself?

_____

_____

_____

_____

_____

_____

_____

2) In what area(s) to you need to be healed to become whole?

_____

_____

_____

_____

_____

Vessels of Honor

_____

_____

_____

3) How do you plan to seek wholeness that only Christ can give?

_____

_____

_____

_____

_____

_____

_____

God will never put something in you that you don't have the ability, power and strength to pull out. It requires courage!

Vessels of Honor

Chapter 4: Pressure on Vessels

In order for you to become a vessel of honor, there will be seasons of your life where you will have to face pressure—emotional pressure, financial pressure, mental pressure and more. It will seem that as soon as you get over one thing, something altogether new will arise and bring on a new form of pressure. There is pressure to become better to meet the standard, to survive the obstacles and more. If you are currently in a season where it seems all hell is breaking loose, before you can get a handle on one thing another thing happens and it feels like every direction you turn something else is happening…don't be alarmed! Calm down! Take a breather! It's supposed to be like this. God is still in control.

Pressure often builds in silence. We have things that we are going through privately, things that are going on in our minds that we can't tell anyone about, things that are so tough to explain that the thought of even sharing them becomes too much to bear. There are so many vessels who are weighed down by hidden, silent and heavy pressure. Slowly and surely, the pressure is rising and building all around and within us.

Merriam Webster defines pressure as, "the weight or force that is produced when something presses or pushes against something else." The key word to me in the definition is *something*. Something is pressing and something is pushing. Have you ever felt like there was something pressing you forward while something else was pushing you back? There are family issues, mistakes, failures, demands to be like someone else, and the demand to live up to other people's expectations and to make other people happy. There is pressure on the job,

Vessels of Honor

pressure at home and pressure at school. Pressure! Have you ever taken several steps forward feeling the press within yourself to want to be better, to do better and to achieve more, when all of a sudden, there is a force of opposition pushing you back? The fact of the matter is; in one form or another; we all currently have or will have pressure against us. Pressure is a part of life.

Vessels of Honor must go through seasons of pressure. An important key to remember about pressure is that everyone goes through it, but everyone doesn't get through it. It takes tenacity, courage and strength to make it through the pressure. I'm not sure if you are aware of it or not, but there's a war going on and you are in the middle of it right now. You are the spoil! There is a strong pull for you to determine what type of vessel you will become.

Raashid K. Brown

On one side is greatness and on the other side is being good. You are the ***"something"*** in the middle. Greatness is what you are destined for, but good is what you are used to. Greatness is your destiny, good is your detriment. Greatness is your future, good is your past. Which one do you choose? Don't answer so quickly. The real answer to this question lies in your actions. It doesn't take much for you to be good, but it does take effort and hard work for you to be great. Anyone can be good, but it takes work and tenacity to be great.

God doesn't want good vessels. He wants great vessels. Great vessels are ones that can be put on display, trusted with huge platforms and notoriety but ultimately the glory will be given to the Maker and Creator of us all. Great vessels can be trusted, have integrity and are willing to submit to His plan, rule and will. Good vessels can be used, but only temporarily. They can't be trusted to be used for long periods of time, because they can't handle the pressure that comes with being great. Good vessels will appear to be great at first, but they will crack under pressure due to not having the sustainability to withstand the pressure.

Please understand that the pressure you are facing right now is indicative of your use later. If God has significant use for you as His Vessel of Honor, there will be great pressure against you for two reasons. The first is because the enemy will try to get you to be so tied down in pressure that you will start to think you have nothing else to give. WRONG! Everything that you have been through, are going through and will go through is part of what will make you into that whole and complete Vessel of Honor that He called and created you to be. It was all factored in. The second reason for the pressure, is it is preparation for what you are to handle later. This pressure that you are facing now is not meant to take you out, it is meant to make you better. Pressure bursts pipes, but it also makes diamonds! You were made to survive the pressure and to live in greatness. Yes, it is a struggle. It's supposed to be. If it was easy, anyone could do it!

    Suicide, depression, various disorders and emotional explosions/implosions are external displays of internal pressure. There are some people that we talk to everyday who appear to be fine on the outside, but the reality is that; internally, they are struggling with pressure. The pressure of living life after the death of a spouse or a divorce, the pressure of having to raise children on a single income, the pressure of having to go to work sick because missing one day of pay could cause the lights to be cut off, the pressure of having to come home to a man who beats you and the pressure of coming home to a wife who verbally and mentally breaks you down. It's not just pressure, its continuous pressure.

Continuous means: for something to be ongoing or unbroken. There are some people who have been living with pressure for a while and it seems too much to bear. There are some who have been dealing and living with the continuous pressure of survival for decades—unbroken pressure. This pressure pushes against your mind, your thoughts, your emotions and your spirit. I'm not talking about the kind of pressure that can be fixed by taking some pain meds. The unbroken pressure that I'm speaking about is the pressure you have been carrying that you can't tell anyone about. The pressure that your kids don't know about, your spouse doesn't know about, your employees don't know about, your friends, your church – no one—knows about this pressure.

There was a joke that kids would play when I was in school. They would take a canned soda and shake it up violently and forcefully. If you were holding it, you could feel the can become tight. The object of the joke was that the person who would get the can would have a mess all over them, because once opened, the contents in the can would come flying out. Why? Because the pressure inside of the can had built up so much that upon opening it, all the carbon released at one time.

Life may have shaken you up over the past few years. Unexpected deaths, failures and unplanned events have caused so much pressure that it seems like everything is falling apart. The pipes of your life feel like they are expanding and one more thing could cause them to explode. Can I tell you something? The pressure you have experienced so far in your life serves a greater purpose! The pressure is not meant to take you out. It's not meant to defeat you. The pressure you are experiencing is making you into the vessel that will give God the most glory.

Again, the same pressure that bursts pipes makes diamonds! A pipe is equipped to handle a certain amount of pressure, much like a diamond is meant to handle a certain type of pressure. The ability to handle the pressure is what determines if you burst or if you become a diamond. The pressure that you are experiencing is indicative of the greatness that is inside of you! You see and feel pressure, but God sees power! The pressure you are facing now is going to be your power later. The power to live past and live through everything that is telling you to be less than who God has called and created you to be.

The only way for your pressure to become your power is to survive the storm. If it was easy, anybody could do it. Life is hard. It's not meant to be easy? It was never promised to you that it would be easy. So, since life isn't easy, we have to find a way to handle it better. Can I make a recommendation to you? Stop focusing on what you are carrying and focus on how you are carrying it. Let me explain what I mean.

One of the fastest ways to severely injure your back is to pick up a heavy object without the correct posture. There is a right way to pick up and carry something that is heavy. Sometimes, it's not that the weight is too heavy. It could be that you aren't carrying it right. Let me go a step further. There are some things that you are not meant to carry. They are not yours; they don't have your name on them. They do not belong to you. It's not your job to carry other people's burdens.

If things are too heavy for you, carry them to God through prayer; earnest prayer, and leave them there. 1 Peter 5:7 (KJV) says, "Cast all your care upon him; for he careth for you." The word *cast* in the Greek language is a verb. A verb denotes action, occurrence or a state of events. Cast means to throw. According to Vines Expository Dictionary, cast means to throw, send and thrust. This scripture literally is saying for you to throw, send and thrust on God, all of the things are pulling on you, distracting you or causing you to have anxiety. How do you do that? Through prayer-- wholehearted, earnest and fervent prayer to God! Why do it? --Because He cares for you. What that means is that He avails Himself to take on your load, and your burden so you don't have to.

He wants to use you as a Vessel of Honor to reach others, but He can't do so because you are being pulled and distracted. There comes a point where you have to stop carrying and start casting. What God wants to accomplish in our world is either being slowed or delayed, people are dying, people are lost and people are searching for hope. You are their hope. Cast your cares on God!

Vessels of Honor

Chapter Appraisal

1) What pressure(s) are you currently facing?

_____

_____

_____

_____

_____

_____

_____

2) What are you carrying that you need to cast off?

_____

_____

_____

_____

_____

3) In what situations has God turned your pressure into power?

The same pressure that bursts pipes also makes diamonds!

Vessels of Honor

Chapter 5: New Wine in Old Skins

As a Vessel of Honor; full of faithfulness and purpose, Jesus was a trend breaker. Knowing who He was, and Who called Him gave Him the confidence to challenge the status quo of the day. The religious people of that day didn't receive Him until after His death, because He broke rules and regulations. When you are a vessel who is fully aware and has the courage to bring forth the treasure inside, you will step over all limits and bounds that have been set by others.

In Mark 2:22(BLB), Jesus said something that arrested my attention. The context of the scripture is Jesus having a conversation with John's disciples and the Pharisees. John's disciples and the Pharisees are interested in knowing why the people who follow Jesus do not do what the other religious people do. In this case, they wanted to know why

Jesus' followers were not fasting when everyone else was. Jesus answered them in three parables. A parable is a short story that has a greater meaning. Mark 2:22 records the last parable which states, "And no one puts new wine into old wineskins; otherwise the wine will burst the wineskins, and the wine will be destroyed—and the wineskins. Instead, new wine is poured into new wineskins."

In order to properly understand what Jesus was saying and the greater meaning behind it, you have to know something about wineskins and the process of making wine in those days. Wine was not made like it is today. No, wine in that day was made by a lot of hard work and was a monotonous task. Grapes had to be crushed so that grape juice could be used. Once the necessary ingredients were gathered, the wine was put into wineskins and capped. Wineskins were goatskins made to carry liquid, which in this case was frequently wine. Wait…if the wineskins were made to carry something, isn't that the same as a vessel? Right!

Once the wine was put into the *vessel* of a wineskin, the wineskin was sealed and set to the side. The process of fermentation would begin. Fermentation is simply the process of a substance breaking down into another substance. The juice, along with other ingredients, would mix together in the wineskin. When the wine was put into the wineskin and sealed, the mixture in the skin would make a gas that would begin to swell until the process of fermentation was complete, thus making wine.

If someone attempted to put new wine into an old wineskin, there was a great chance that the old wineskin would burst, due to it not being able to stretch and expand during the fermentation process.

What does all that mean in contrast to what Jesus was saying? Here's the answer. Jesus was telling John's disciples and the Pharisees that the gospel Jesus was preaching was not able to be received by the religious leaders of that day. Jesus preached and manifested Himself to people who were able to be stretched and expanded. The people who were following Jesus were new *vessels* and could receive and grow with the new *wine*.

When I read this scripture, the Lord began to speak to me concerning us as *vessels* today. The wine that is being poured into vessels is not just the Holy Spirit, although that is a MUST HAVE for all believers. I believe that God wants to pour new ideas, new plans, fresh visions and fresh prospective into you. He has new concepts for business, new ways to enrich the life you have, new ways to reach people and new jobs. He wants to do greater works

Vessels of Honor

and give you greater levels of influence. The issue is, can you expand enough to receive it all?

God wants vessels He can pour newness into -- newness that is attractive in gathering others, but also maintains a standard that would ultimately give Him the glory. It's not that God isn't ready; the issue is that He doesn't use vessels who can't be trusted to maintain and hold the weight of His glory without breaking. If you break; which means become destroyed due to not being able to stretch, then what He put inside of your would be wasted. The treasure inside you is too valuable to be wasted.

Wineskins, in Biblical days; much like wine bottles of today, were made to be filled. Those vessels were not made for ambience. Vessels were made to contain, hold and carry something. The price of the wine is not so much about the vessel itself, but about what is inside the vessel. As

Raashid K. Brown

I have stated several times now, there is a treasure inside you! That treasure has power, strengths, and abilities that you have not tapped into. God pours into you through the form of creative ideas, innovative concepts and helping you make the correct decisions. His pour is meant to mix with what is locked in your treasure. When His pour and your treasure start to mix, swelling will take place. Swelling will be uncomfortable. In fact, one of the main ways you can tell you are swelling will be discomfort.

People who have been around you for years will say, "You are starting to act different!" Congrats! You've started swelling! Swelling is necessary for you to become the vessel that He wants you to be. You have to do it! God doesn't pour anything into you that He doesn't want to be poured out to others. If He put it in you, He wants

Vessels of Honor

it to be poured out. Jesus poured Himself out on the cross so that you could be filled! Now it's your time, and your responsibility to pour out what is inside of you so that others can be filled as well. What should be poured out is only what God put in, not what you have picked up or have received from someone else.

As a rule, that's why you don't have to beg people to stay in your life. If; for some reason, someone wants to walk out of your life because they do not see the treasure inside of you, let them go. People who walk with you closely should be able to expand and stretch during different times in order to remain active in your life. It's not meant for everyone to behold your treasure. Your treasure was meant for specific people in certain places. The key to becoming effective is finding the right people for your treasure. There are some people who are meant to pour into you to keep you full, and there are some people who are meant to benefit from you pouring into them.

If you die full because you refused to pull from your treasure and pour out to others, then you have missed your purpose. Vessels were made to be filled, but they were not made to be filled forever. How can others "taste and see that the Lord is good" (Psalm 34:8) if you die full? For people to taste of God, who is the One that makes the wine and pours it into us, He wants you to start emptying out. Write the book, get the degree, mentor, volunteer, build, organize it, grow it, do whatever it takes for you to pour out. People who have become and will become the greatest among us are those who have found their treasure and begin to pour out.

Vessels of Honor

The more you pour out, the more He pours in. God will not pour into something that is always full. That would be equivalent to me pouring water into a glass that is already filled. What would be the point? The only thing that happens then is that the new water is wasted. God will not waste His blessing. It's too valuable and too meaningful to be wasted! The wine that was necessary in the 90's has changed into the wine needed in the 21st century. What worked then is not going to work now. That's why tradition, doing the same thing that used to be done, is an enemy to God. Some people are still walking around with old wine in them. It was good at one point, but He has something new that will cause you to become more relevant and more effective. The issue is not that you are a bad vessel who can't be used. You could be a good vessel; you are just carrying old wine that is not effective in this season.

Vessels of Honor

Chapter Appraisal

1) In what ways have you started to stretch and expand?

_____

_____

_____

_____

_____

_____

2) What 'newness' has God been pouring into you?

_____

_____

_____

_____

3) In what ways have you started to pour out? What initiatives or actions have you taken to do so?

A Vessel of Honor is one who is made uncomfortable; through expanding and stretching, to receive the "newness" God has for them.

Chapter 6: Available Vessels

As I stated in the first chapter, we live in a world where vessels are used every day. Although there are many vessels, how many vessels are actually available to be used? Sometimes vessels can become so occupied, busy and tied up doing other things, holding other people's visions, dreams, goals and aspirations that they fail to truly carry their own. It would be a waste for the treasure inside you to die in you, because you spent so much of your life being available for other people or occupied by other things. What if you failed to become available for what is inside of you?

It's imperative that you are available to be used at any time. Why? So that God can use you at any time, place or opportunity. That is actually the goal of our walk and relationship with Christ on the Earth. When He wants something to be done, we should desire to become the one He knows is dependable to use. We must never allow ourselves to become people who are used "every once in a while," such as every Sunday, once every month, once every conference or once every day. No! We ought to be available for use every day and at every second. God wants to reach the world, but He chooses to do it through you.

Often times we get upset with God, because we feel we aren't being used like we could be. We see others functioning, moving and doing things all around us while we may be having the same zeal and aren't being used. I'll admit, I went through a season of that myself. I kept trying to figure out why someone; with less passion than me, was being used, while I was sitting waiting for an opportunity. The reason is that I was really not available.

Vessels of Honor

Being available goes beyond being present for the moment. Being available is about being present for the preparation, the development and the growth. We need to be available for every step along the way that leads us to our moment uniting us with our destiny. So many times we want to be available for the moment, but we have failed to plan for the moment. Preparation and development are key! Although the moment may be there in the days to come, a truly honorable vessel will spend time in preparation for those moments.

Let's say that you are expectantly waiting for your moment of marriage. While you are waiting for the right person to come along, an honorable vessel would be ensuring that they are developing in every way to be suitable for a spouse. An honorable vessel would be getting their finances together, fixing issues of their past, and getting their life together so that when their "moment" comes they will be ready to embrace it. Embrace it with the certainty that they can securely hold on to what they have been waiting for.

Another example would be expectantly awaiting and wanting your moment of leadership. In spite of what many of us have been told, leadership does not start the moment you start leading. Leadership begins the moment you start following. While you are waiting for your leadership moment, a Vessel of Honor would be submitted to the authority of someone else; developing and sharpening the leadership skills they already have. They would be exposing themselves to different things so that when their moment comes, they will be groomed to embrace the moment.

Vessels of Honor

Life has a way of preparing you for big moments that you don't even know are coming. One of the best ways life prepares us for our "moment" in the future is through challenges, situations, storms and chaos. Pressure! These events aren't there to take us out. No, in fact, these are events developing us for the "moment" that is coming! Some things need to die within us while others need awakening for the next step in the journey.

The storms, challenges and chaos in our lives are our gym where we develop muscles that will enable us to be strong and to fully embrace our moment of availability when it comes. If you quit or fail to grow through your storm, you will have done something terrible. You will stop your development. Stopping your development is a travesty that is taking place around us far more than we think. So many people have given up hope and have severely hindered their development.

Let me be transparent and share a moment in my life when a storm came unexpectedly. In 2015, my marriage failed and I found myself to be part of the first time marriage statistics ending in divorce. This storm was something that I did not see coming, although my actions prior to the divorce indicated that it was inevitable. This storm produced such tumultuous chaos for me mentally, emotionally and spiritually that there were moments when I didn't know if I would make it through. Have you ever gone through something so painful that you hid to disguise the pain, the circumstances and the agony so that people would not know your reality? Have you ever had someone ask you, "How are you doing?" and because you could not muster the

Vessels of Honor

strength to really tell them, you settled for the casual, "I'm fine?"

This particular storm lasted for about two months. I know what it is to hide my brokenness so that others can't see who I really am and what I'm really going through. I was like a clown who uses paint to make himself part of the circus entertainment. Have you ever had to put on an "entertainment" face to show the world you are making it? That nothing can break you, and that you are in complete control of everything; when in actuality, you go home at night and can't sleep because you are secretly hurting? It's chaotic. Often times we tend to look differently at people who display their chaos externally through drug abuse, sex, alcoholism, repetitive problematic relationships, bouts of depression, anxiety and other forms of external display. We can see them crying out for help. We should be just as concerned about the individuals who are suffering silently every day. These individuals are doing everything they always do, but bleeding privately. That; in fact, was me.

See, there are some situations that may come up in your life that will knock you down to your knees. There are some things that will come up in your life; unexpectedly, that will leave you gasping for air. There are some situations that will come knocking at your door that will have you trying everything to compensate for the pain you feel. These are the storms, situations and chaos that I'm talking about. Things, that when you start talking about them, bring tears from the hurt that is buried in the pain of your heart. Those tears slide across the bridge of your nose, because of the memories of what you did privately to compensate for the pain.

Vessels of Honor

About two months after my storm; while I was having a bleeding moment and wallowing in my pain, I decided to come face to face with my storm. I decided that I wasn't going to continue to run from it, hide it or paint on any more faces. I stood face to face with it. What I didn't know was, that my storm and my chaos, wanted to partner with me. The feelings I was having prior to confronting my storm were just that. They were my refusal to look at my reality and accept it for what it was. Once I confronted it and faced it, I realized that the storm actually wanted to help me.

Slowly but surely, I started to partner with my storm. I began to look at my mistakes, my failures and my shortcomings; I examined myself. That was the key beginning stage of development for me. We often run from the examination, because that is the point where we have to face our decisions that got us into the storms. If we will be honest with ourselves, every storm in our life is not related to cold weather and warm weather mixing. The external things are beyond our control. Some storms are; in fact, because we have created them for ourselves.

After I finished examining myself, I embraced my storm as the avenue for my development and not my detriment. I took control of the storm rather than letting the storm take control of me! It was then that my storm and I partnered together. What I didn't realize was that my storm; which was hot and cold at times, was making me into the vessel that I needed to be. I didn't see it coming!

Another amazing thing that I didn't see coming was that my storm helped to make me available. How? Because I learned from my storm, what things I needed to change in order for me to become an honorable vessel. I learned how to be fully aware of decisions so as not to become a vessel that sabotaged myself from the better things in life due to poor decisions. Vessels make mistakes; they don't get everything right all the time. We fall short, but the great thing about true Vessels of Honor is, that they will not break! Vessels of Honor are survivors who have the innate ability to come out stronger on the other side.

    Some of you are waiting; looking for the strength and courage within you to confront the issues of your past. Your issues don't want to fight you; they want to help make you available. These issues keep coming up, because you need to address them. Often; in our ignorance, we suppress these things. We think that if we overlook them, they will go away. That is not the case. The issues that keep arising from within are hints from God, telling you that you have to address these things; so that when your moment comes, you will be ready.

Could it be that our moment is oh so close to us? But because we have not dealt with or healed from our past, we will not be available to embrace it for what it will yield? But because of the issues of our past, we will not be available to embrace it? Our moment may not come in a manner we expect. Could it be that our moment will come in a way that will resemble a moment in our past? That's why it is important that we deal with our past issues. Our moment could be staring at us right in the face, but we are overlooking it due to what will be new resembling something that looks old.. But because it may be camouflaged in something that we have associated with pain, we will miss it. What you have been waiting for is around the corner. It's

Vessels of Honor

moving closer to you. It's searching for you, like you are for it. Are you available?

Chapter Appraisal

1) What are some things that are causing you not to be available for your moment?

_____

_____

_____

_____

_____

_____

2) What storms did you have to partner with in order to survive?

_____

_____

_____

_____

_____

Vessels of Honor

_____

_____

3) As a leader, what/who are you currently leading and what/who are you currently following?

_____

_____

_____

_____

_____

_____

God wants to reach the world, and He wants to do it through you!

Vessels of Honor

Chapter 7: Loyalty

While there are many factors that come to mind that a Vessel of Honor must embrace in order to be used to their highest and best use, there is something specific that the Lord impressed upon me. God is in search of something among us that is rare to find anywhere in the world. This one treasure is so valuable, so precious and important to God that; according to Scripture, He vows to reveal the power of His right hand to those who possess it. The amazing aspect of this thought is that God is all-knowing, all-powerful and omnipresent, but yet He is searching for something.

Jesus Himself possessed this treasure; and because of it, He gave up His life to save you and me. Let me go a step further. This one treasure is something that has been missing from our homes, our careers, our communities, our nation and even our churches. It's missing in our personal, spiritual and social relationships. Some people have established structures and organizations that will ultimately fail due to neither party having this one thing. It is something not taught in school. It isn't something you can go to the store and buy. It isn't something you can order online. The one thing I'm speaking about is loyalty.

There's a story recorded in 2 Chronicles 16 that I would like to extract some principles from to assist in our understanding of loyalty. This particular story records the demise of a king. King Asa was the third king of Judah and the fifth king in the lineage of David. He was the great-great grandson of King David and the great grandson of Solomon (who, according to Scripture, is the wisest man who ever lived).

Vessels of Honor

When Asa came into his kingship, he was regarded as a good and righteous king in the sight of God. In the early years of his reign, a large army, believed to be a one-million-man army, rose up against him. He had an army, but it was less than 600,000. After taking battle positions, Asa prayed to God for help prior to the battle (2 Chronicles 14:11). God honored Asa's prayer and struck their enemy, giving Asa the victory. The Spirit of God came upon a prophet by the name of Azariah and told Asa that the Lord was with him. Azariah prophesied to Asa giving Asa promises from God. One thing he said was, "If you seek him, he will be found by you, but if you forsake him, he will forsake you" (2 Chronicles 15:2).

The reason Asa was victorious in a battle where the adversity against him was great, was because of his loyalty to God. Once he got through the battle, the Lord confirmed him by raising up a prophet to tell Asa that if he would seek Him, God would be found. As long as Asa sought the Lord and remained loyal to Him, God would be there for him as He was in times past. The key condition to the promise was loyalty.

After hearing this amazing prophecy and winning against such adversity, Asa removed idols from the land of Judah and repaired the altar of the Lord. He summoned a great assembly of people and offered up great worship in the form of sacrifices to establish a covenant with God. In their worship, the people took an oath to God that whoever did not seek the Lord God would be killed, no matter how small or great they were (2 Chronicles 15:13).

I want to interject something the Holy Spirit told me to tell you. Often; after great moments of victory, success, and great moments in worship or even after overcoming huge hurdles and obstacles, we make vows to God about things that we are going to change or do differently. Some say, "Lord, if you do this or if you get me out of this, I will do this for you." God; in His faithfulness and care toward us, comes through for us. He makes a way, He lifts up and He tears down. He does His part. Can you say that you are doing yours? Have you stuck to the vow that you made?

Let's fast forward 36 years in Asa's life. 2 Chronicles 16 details that Baasha, King of Israel, attacked Judah. Instead of seeking God like he had done in the past, Asa made a treaty with Ben-Hadad, King of Aram. King Asa went to another person to make provisions for him to win the battle rather than seeking God. Remember, 36 years ago he sought God and was awarded victory, received a prophecy, and even offered great worship. But as time passed; when he was placed in a battle, he sought the help of someone else rather than seeking God.

The interesting thing about this battle is that Asa won. He didn't seek God, but he still won the battle. However Hanani (a seer) went to Asa and told him, "Because you went for help to the King of Aram and didn't ask God for help, you've lost a victory over the army of King Aram (2 Chronicles 16:7). Did you notice what happened? Asa won the battle, but he lost the victory. He won the battle by having his enemy stop waging war with him; however, he lost the victory, which was to overtake his enemy. The consequence of being out of the will of God or moving through things without seeking God's counsel prior to engaging, is that you could win the battle against something, but not gain the victory over it.

What do you do when you win the battle, but lose the victory? Many times we have won the battle in so many different areas, but we still don't have the victory. The problem with winning the battle and losing the victory is that your enemy is silenced, but not destroyed. So many times, we have silent enemies who are still lurking around us in many different ways. They don't remain silent forever. They will start to speak. It's not until we gain the victory over our enemies that they are destroyed. Victory only comes through Christ!

Hannai goes on to tell Asa that the Cushites and the Libyans would come against him with more superior forces. Asa asked God for help and won the victory. A clause in verse 9 is the focus of this chapter. It says, "For the eyes of the Lord run to and fro throughout the whole earth, to shew himself strong in the behalf of them whose heart is perfect towards him." The word "perfect" here does not mean without fault or without error as we're used to hearing it. The Hebrew word for perfect is translated as *shalem* (Strong's Concordance 8003). *Shalem* literally means whole, complete or entire. What this verse is literally saying is that eyes of the Lord run back and forth throughout the whole earth, so that He can show Himself strong on their behalf, for those whose heart is completely and entirely devoted to Him.

Asa was loyal in times past. God made a way for him. The issue that arose was that Asa forgot about his loyalty to God. He started making loyalty agreements with others. He created an idol in others and ran to a king for protection rather than depending of the King of Kings. As a result of losing the victory, Asa also because lame in his feet. What is happening to many people now is that when we become lame in our feet, or mobility as it relates to reaching our destiny, our inheritance is delayed. We can't walk correctly or take divinely ordered steps when we have an infection in our spiritual feet. We could be living decades and still have bad spiritual feet.

As a Vessel of Honor, we must find ourselves being loyal to the things, plans and ways of God so that we can be used to God's highest purpose. Asa was used, but was not able to reach his full potential due to his failure to have his heart entirely devoted to God. As a vessel, sometimes we have to check our devotion level. It is possible to become more committed to people, places, our own vision, goals and dreams than to the will of God. Secretly, many of us have made idols out of mentors, business partners, associates and close friends. We have secretly made "treaties" (like Asa) with others to get us to the next level. As it was with King Asa, so it will be with us.

We don't ever want to be known as vessels who win the battle, but lose the victory. Vessels of Honor are victorious. They walk in victory; decree victory as well. They rest, rule and abide in victory. If you are not obtaining and living in victory in your life, check to ensure that you are actually living as a Vessel of Honor. Have you made secret treaties with people? Maybe not with an individual, but have you conspired with your failures, mistakes, short-comings, proclivities, secret issues and struggles? It may not be something that everyone can see or identify, but you know where you have secretly made a treaty. Vessel; don't win the battle, but lose the victory.

Vessels of Honor

Merriam Webster defines loyal as "unswerving in allegiance, faithful to a private person to whom fidelity is due and faithful to a cause, ideal custom, institution or product." Three words in this definition immediately stood out to me--allegiance, faithful and fidelity. These three words speak to a commitment and strong union between people, places or things. A lot of what we know as loyalty isn't loyalty at all. What we are seeing a lot of today is simply convenient attachments. When the situation or circumstance stops being convenient, then our "loyalty" to a person, place or thing stops. Being loyal transcends feelings and emotions. Being loyal is a matter of the heart, not of convenience.

Chapter Appraisal

1) How is your loyalty to God?

2) In what ways could you become more loyal to God?

Vessels of Honor

3) Have you ever experienced seasons of infection due to being disobedient and disloyal to God? Explain.

_____

_____

_____

_____

_____

_____

Don't win the battle and lose the victory!

Chapter 8: Vessels Must Be Empty

Vessels of many different forms are used every day. What matters most is the availability of the vessel. It's one thing to be a vessel, but it means something altogether different for the vessel to be available for use. The time is ever so confirming that there is a famine in our world for vessels to effect change for the Kingdom of God. In this chapter, I will expound upon the concept that; in order for you (the vessel) to be used, you must be empty.

Being empty is something that seems so simplistic in nature; but in reality, it is one of the most difficult things to be and maintain. So many individuals are dealing with silent frustration. The frustration stems from seeing others function, move and even embrace their calling, purpose and destiny. At the same time, some of us sit on the sidelines waiting for our chance to be used. We have spent so much time in preparation and making the necessary sacrifices that is seems as though our chance to step into our own should be evident. For those dealing with the silent frustration of seeing others move while waiting on your chance, this chapter is for you.

One of the reasons why you haven't been called into action is, because you are not empty. Your mind, your heart and your spirit have some things inside that have taken up residence. Things such as bitterness, jealousy, secret addictions and deep wounds haven't been treated or healed within your heart. They are still present in the deep recesses of your heart, beneath the calling and gift and tucked into a corner. It's that issue that you haven't confronted that is making you not available.

Vessels of Honor

Deep down; in the recess of your heart, there's something that you have to deal with in order for you to be used.

The issue is not if God wants to use you. He does! There are people, places and issues in the world waiting for the manifestation of who you are. There's no one else who can offer them what you can offer them. God wants to use you; however, what He will not do is expose you to them yet because you are not empty. You may be available as it relates to time, but that is not the issue. You can have all the time in the world. But if the deep hidden things aren't dealt with, you are still not available for use.

There is something else; other than hidden issues in our mind, hearts and souls that will cause us not to be empty. This one thing is actually what is holding a lot of people back. This one thing; if you've noticed, will allow you to only go so far before you are abruptly pulled back. The one thing that I'm speaking about is **sin**.

Sin is anything that separates us from the will of God for our lives. The Bible lays out a foundation of what our lives as Christians are supposed to look like. We are the reflection of Christ in the Earth. When we have hidden struggles and sin in our lives that we are not seeking deliverance from, we hinder our own availability. Despite what people may say, deliverance is real and it is something that you can have and maintain! You don't have to struggle with it, carry it, hide it or secretly do anything. The power of God is available to set you free and to break every chain that is keeping you attached to those things with which you struggle.

Vessels of Honor

I'd like to interject a scripture text and story to show the importance of empty vessels. In 2 Kings: 4, a story is recorded of a woman whose husband has died; and as a result, the wife is left with debt. The woman cries out to the prophet Elisha saying that the creditor was coming to take her two sons. According the Mosaic Law, servitude through family for the means of resolving a debt was lawful up until the year of Jubilee (Exodus 21:1-2, Leviticus 25:39-41 and Deuteronomy 15:1-11). Can you imagine the frustration and the pain of this woman? Her husband died. She was a widow. She had to deal with sleeping in a bed alone. She had to deal with the emotional pain of not having her companion to talk to who was once readily available. She had to deal with parenting alone now. On top of all the physiological and emotional pain that she had to endure, she was hit with another issue—the lack of money.

This woman was crying out from a place of reaching her wit's end. She must have been emotionally exhausted, physically tired and physiologically out of control. Elisha asked the woman two questions in verse 2: "How can I help you? What do you have in your house?" Those two questions alone are enough to write a book about. His first question came about as a result of hearing her problem. Saying, "How can I help you?" was Elisha becoming a vessel to serve this woman in her time of need. He was given purpose as a vessel in that moment to address her needs. Is there someone around you right now to whom you could become a vessel? Maybe it's not a person. It might be a place, a situation or a business. The place where you have a passion to serve is where you are needed as a vessel.

Elisha's second question to the woman was, "What is in your house?" This question startled me. Knowing that this lady was a widow; she was in debt, and that the creditors were currently on their way to take her sons, I thought Elisha was going to offer a solution to her problem. He would have been right to pray for manna to fall from heaven, pray for people to come and give her the money she needed, or pray that her debt would be erased by her creditors. As a matter of fact, I can tell you exactly what was in her house—fear, frustration, hurt, emotional turmoil and grief. This woman was being torn every which way. She was caught and pulled into several directions all at the same time. Have you ever felt like everything was falling apart at the same time? Have you ever felt like when one thing fell apart, everything else started falling apart? If you have, you can relate to how this woman felt.

Her first response to him was, "Your handmaid doesn't have anything in the house." What was in the house was nothing that she wanted to claim. There's nothing there. Her perception was that there was no value in her house. If this woman was like any woman in today's world, she knew exactly what was in her house. She knew where things were, when they were out of place, when something wasn't right and even when someone had been there. She tells the prophet, there's nothing there "except a pot of oil." Oil had many different uses. It could be used in lamps to provide light, it could be used for heat, it could be used for cooking and it was used as a symbol of anointing (both ceremonially and for the healing of the sick). Based on the needs of what it could be used for, oil was valuable. The word "pot" was transliterated from the word "jar" or "flask." Basically, the woman had a jelly jar of oil left.

After hearing what she has, Elisha tells the woman, in verses 3 and 4, to go around to all of her neighbors and borrow empty vessels. How does a woman in debt, whose creditors are on the way, have the courage to go into deeper debt by borrowing anything from anyone? Her problem was made worse before it was made better. She got into more debt while in debt. She got into more trouble while in trouble. She got into more chaos while in chaos. Have you ever felt like things got worse before they got better? Have you ever been in a dilemma, when another dilemma arose? The difference in this debt as opposed to her previous one is that she was being set up for something. If your problems, situations, circumstances or issues seem to becoming worse before they're better, you are being set up! Sometimes things have to be in a certain position, in a certain state of chaos or on a certain level of dysfunction, so when things do change for the better, no one will get the glory for this situation but God alone. So that when it's time for you to come up and out, no one will get the glory for this situation; but God! In fact, God does His best work in chaos. When things are without form; appearing as a waste, void, empty, dark or obscure, know that it's a setup! When God steps in, things have to change. His presence alone brings light, fullness, joy and peace. If that is where you are, invite Him in!

What qualified the vessels that were sitting in her neighbor's homes as good for use was that the vessels were empty. The vessels had a purpose, but the purpose was not for the home that they were

Vessels of Honor

in. Sometimes; as vessels, we can be sitting; not being used to our highest and best use all because we aren't in the right house. The place isn't always physical. In fact; most of the time, the place where we are most filled is in our hearts, minds and souls. Toxic and unhealthy relationships have caused us to become full of stuff that has weighed us down, but the stuff is not conducive for us to be used. This widow had one assignment, and that was to go borrow vessels that were empty.

After she got the vessels, the widow was informed to go inside her house and shut the door behind "you and your sons" (verse 4). The place where grief, frustration and fear resided is where the woman was told to go back. This time, she went back with more trouble than she came out with. This time she was in more debt, because she had borrowed empty vessels.

The last thing Elisha told the woman was "pour out into all those vessels, and thou shalt set aside that which is full." He told her, "From the one jar that you have, pour out into the empty vessels and once they are filled set them aside."

Verse 6 says that as the woman started pouring oil from her jelly jar into the borrowed vessels; her jelly jar never ran out of oil. As long as there was an empty vessel, a need, she had enough oil in her jar to fill it. The story doesn't say how big or how small the other jars were. Truthfully, it really doesn't matter. What mattered most was that there were empty vessels. As long as there was a need in the form of an empty vessel, there was a flow of oil present. Again, oil was used in that day for lighting, cooking and anointing. The oil that she had present from the start of the story was all that she needed. What was missing was the empty vessels?

Vessel, are you empty? If not, this would be a great time for you to start to pour out those things that are taking up residence in your life, your heart, your mind and in your spirit that are blocking you from being empty.

The reason why you have to be empty is, because God wants to use you as a conduit of His power and anointing. A conduit is a channel for conveying water, wiring or other items. A conduit serves as a covering and protector for what has to flow through it. Conduits are usually hidden. When you walk into a house or a building; generally, the conduits are hidden behind walls. They aren't meant to be seen, but they have to be present so that whatever is flowing through them reaches the intended destination.

God places us in certain environments, places and atmospheres, so that His power and His glory can flow through us wherever we are. You are His conduit in those places. If you are not empty, He can't flow! The devil knows this. In fact, the strategy of the enemy is to get you angry, upset, and frustrated or out of focus when you are in those places where God wants to flow through you. The place where you experience the most frustration, is the place that God wants to use you as the conduit of His power and His glory. The enemy isn't fighting just you; he's fighting against the flow of God's power and glory that should always be flowing through you. His glory and power should flow through you like water flows through pipes inside of a structure. You are His conduit. Don't stop the flow. He's fighting against the oil that's in you. Don't stop the flow.

Vessels of Honor

There's a need for oil in your life. The oil will light up the dark nights that are soon to come. The oil will heal and soothe those broken places in your life that nobody knows about. The secret addictions, secret affairs and secret lives that no one knows you are living, are hindering you from receiving the oil and from being a conduit of God's power and glory. The oil will slide right down to the place where you are broken and fix the cracks in your armor. YOU NEED THE OIL! Pour out! Pour out! Vessel, you must be empty.

I once heard a story about a gentleman named James who lived in a small town. Although James was loved by the people, he was an extremely lazy employee. One faithful customer came into the store. The customer didn't see James so he inquired of the store owner, "Hey, where's James?" "Oh, he retired," the store owner replied.

The customer said, "Oh wow! Well, good for him. What are you going to do to fill his vacancy?" The owner looked at the customer and said, "James didn't leave any vacancy."

You may not be a lazy employee, but will there be a vacancy left when you leave your areas of influence? Your purpose as a vessel of honor is to let your light shine so brightly in those areas; that when you are not present, there is a vacancy. In fact, God has planted in you what is needed to make those environments better. He has placed you right there. The frustration that you are experiencing may be to prevent you from becoming who you need to be in the environment you are in. If you do not produce fruit, let your light shine or be effective, you will not leave a vacancy.

We were not created just to do something for God. We are destined to contain God. A Vessel

Vessels of Honor

of Honor is the only container God uses on a perpetual basis to do His work and His will. In fact, they are the only ones qualified to be used! God is not just satisfied when we do something for Him. After all, He did give His life. What we do is only what is required. What God wants is containers for His power and glory!

So many individuals; especially young people, are searching for fulfillment and for something to fill up their life. Like me, they spend so much time chasing after things, doing things and experimenting with things, hoping that whatever they are doing will fill them up. However; at the end of their searching, they are left empty. The emptiness is often magnified after every new experience that ends in nothing. We may be gratified but never satisfied. The issue is not that we are empty. We've learned earlier that being empty is a good thing! The real issue is that what you may be attempting to fill yourself with is not suitable for who you really are. The only thing meant to satisfy and fill the emptiness inside of you is God!

Education, religion, marriage, sex, traveling, money and all the things that we think we need will not fill us up. They mean nothing. No matter how good we think these things are they will not fill you up. Nothing can fill a man up and satisfy him, but God Himself. Nothing can fill a woman and satisfy her, but God Himself. That's why it's essential that you make it a habit to get into the presence of God and let Him fill you up. So many of us are full of material things and fleshly desires. The fleshly desires will never be satisfied. Our flesh will always want more, need more and seek out more. If you ever get fully into the presence of God, you will

Vessels of Honor

see that what you've been in need of for years, He can supply in minutes.

Many times; when something new is released, the public is raving about it and wanting it. The manufacturer can't keep up with the demand. Their supply is limited to what is available and was predicated based upon the demand of the item. Fortunately, God does not have this problem. As long as you have a demand of Him to fill you up, He has the supply! He is limitless and non-exhaustible.

Chapter Appraisal

1) What is something you know you need to let go off to become empty?

_____
_____
_____
_____
_____
_____

2) In what areas have you stopped the flow of God in your family, workplace, church and home?

_____
_____
_____
_____

Vessels of Honor

_____

_____

3) Specifically, where would you like God to fill you?

_____

_____

_____

_____

_____

_____

Bloom right where God has you!

Vessels of Honor

Chapter 9: Vessels Must be Developed

Many factors tend to effect young, emerging and innovative leaders rising to power. No doubt, these individuals are vessels who have the potential to change the world. God has released so many great things in seed form into the lives of the millennial generation. So much so, that it will take two generations after us before we truly see what it is that God has put inside of us. Things that people have spent years of education, thousands of dollars, countless hours and years to gain, God has released to us. We have the dexterity, skill, knowledge and power in us for such a time as this. Although you are gifted, talented and have what it takes to get the job done, there is something else that you need.

For you to make the impact that you were called to make and to become who it is God has called; created and purposed you to be, you must go through a season of development. Anyone who has ever reached a high level of what we deem as "success" had to go through a season of development. Development is what prepares you to occupy the place you are destined for. Development is tedious; it can be mundane and it can feel as if it is unnecessary, but it is required.

Before we go any further, I'd like to define what develop means so that we can have an accurate definition of what it is we need to become who we are called to be. **Develop is defined as situations, circumstances and teachings that bring out your capabilities and possibilities.** Anything that has the potential to bring out what is inside of you is your development--good, bad, right, wrong, ups and downs.

Vessels of Honor

There are two words in the definition that make "develop" oxymoronic—situations and circumstance. Generally, when we think of situations and circumstances our minds think about what it is we; individually, have been through. Those negative things, that when they come to mind, cause our hearts to still ache: The relationships that failed, the business deal that didn't go through and the promotion that was promised to you but you never received. The phone call that greeted you with bad news, the molestation, the unexpected death, the unexplained departure, the loneliness, the sadness, the grief and the frustration. The list goes on and on. All of us may not have suffered the same situation, but we have all endured situations and circumstances that have caused us a lot of pain.

Those negative situations serve a greater purpose in your life. Yes, they did hurt. No, it wasn't right. No! It didn't and still doesn't feel good, but it serves a purpose. The purpose of what you went through was not to take you out, but to make you better. Those are the places where you are the most developed. Good times have a way of helping us. But if you want to really be developed; it's through trying times that weigh us down and are uncomfortable, that we become who we have been called, created, purposed and destined to be.

When athletes go to the gym to prepare for the season to come, they use a series of machines and heavy weights to condition their bodies for the impact the upcoming season will bring. Athletes must endure some hurt and some painful workout sessions; but the end result, is that they will be ready for the upcoming season. Without

Vessels of Honor

conditioning, they wouldn't be ready nor probably of much use. Development is necessary.

If someone wanted to make a chair out of a piece of wood, it wouldn't be profitable to use tissue paper to smooth the surface. The tissue paper would tear due to the surface of the wood being gritty and grainy. In order to produce a smooth surface that will benefit the customer who will buy it, the craftsman must use sandpaper. Sandpaper is an abrasive material with grit and sand stuck to it. The gritty sand attached to the paper is swiped against the wood on the table to produce a smoother layer that is beneficial to what the craftsman had in mind. The wood is good alone. But in order for it to be used properly, it must be developed.

As it is with the athlete and the wood, so it is with you and I. God has a way of using things that seem to be heavy, tough, and rough to smooth us into vessels that can be used to His highest and best use. Often; during tough times, what we tend to do is quit. We stop, turn around and run away from the battle, situation, circumstance or problem to safeguard our feelings and emotions. It's human nature. If we know something is going to hurt us, we tend to do whatever it takes to keep us from facing that painful situation. Quitting seems best at the time. Those things that we are running away from are things that come to develop us into what and who it is that we need to be. That's your sandpaper! That is what God is going to use to smooth you out.

Suppose the craftsman of the wood table never used the sandpaper. Do you know what could happen? The person who uses the table runs the risk of getting a splinter. The table then becomes dangerous for anyone to use because it could possibly cause injury and discomfort. That is the same thing that can happen to you if you run from the development; the sand paper. You become a hazard to people around you. Your attitude, your emotions, your personality and your speech will be giving "splinters" to those around you. After a while, you will find you are by yourself. Those closest to you start to realize that you are more of a hazard than a help to them.

Instead of looking at our situations and circumstances as pitfalls, let's change our perspective and embrace them as pit stops. The only way that a struggle can become a pitfall rather than a pit stop, is if you avoid facing the circumstance or situation. A pitfall is a trap that is meant to keep you locked out and hold you hostage, to prevent you from reaching your God-given and ordained destiny. It's a snag that lingers, a stumbling block that you refuse to climb over and a risk that you refuse to take. It's what is keeping you from purposely pressing forward. It may hurt, you may have to cry, you may have to sweat and you may have to be upset; but square your shoulders, hold your chest out and face your issue!

For the sake of clarity, let me explain the anatomy of what a pit stop is. In motorsport races, drivers often pull over into pit stops for a variety of reasons. Tires blow out, gas is low, adjustments are needed on the car, a driver changes, or the grill of the car is dirty. A pit stop is equivalent to what anyone does when taking a long-distance trip somewhere. The purpose of the pit stop is to get the vehicle in good working order, so that it can safely get back on the road to either complete the race or make it to the intended destination. The pit stop is not meant as a place to linger. It's meant for you to get what you need or do what you need to do in order to get back on the road.

When it comes to the things that you have been through or are currently going through, take the time to assess if you are at a pitfall or a pit stop. If you haven't moved forward, then you are at a pitfall. If you can take the lesson as well as the pain and keep moving, you are ready to exit the pit stop and get back on the road to reach your destiny.

The Bible says it like this: "Count it all joy, my brethren, when ye fall into diver's temptations; knowing this, that the trying of your faith worketh patience. But let patience have her perfect work, that ye may be perfect and entire wanting nothing" James 1:4(KJV). When you are faced with various trials, circumstances, discomforts, calamities and testing, count it as joy. Look at it from the right perspective, knowing that the trying of your faith works patience. Just like the athlete in the gym is working out, the testing and trials of your faith is working out patience. The word patience here doesn't mean waiting around or slowly moving. The original word written in Greek is *hupomone,'* which means endurance and steadfastness. Every situation and circumstance serves a purpose!

The verse goes on to say, "let patience have her perfect work." Let endurance and steadfastness, produced by circumstances and situations, complete what they are supposed to do. They serve a purpose! Why? "That you may be perfect and entire, wanting nothing." Your development is attached to your situation and circumstance. Don't quit on your development. It's not meant to be a pitfall, but a pit stop that produces endurance in you so you can be developed into the great individual

Vessels of Honor

God has called, created, purposed and destined for you to be.

God doesn't want to just have you, he wants to use you! He wants to be able to place you in certain places to be His hands and His arms to pull people closer to Him. He wants to use you to His highest and best use! The plans that He has for you aren't mediocre, small or average. The plans that He has for you and for your life will defy odds, break records and set new standards. These things and many more are a snap shot of what is ahead for you.

The question then becomes, are you ready to be developed for where it is that you are destined to go? You can't make it to your next level undeveloped. It's too risky, and the world doesn't need any more hateful, spiteful and weak people in leadership. You need to be smoothed out and shined; so that when the right people are ready for you and the right opportunity is present to you, there will be no doubt that you are the right person for the job. Vessel, you must be developed!

Vessels of Honor

Chapter Appraisal

1) In what areas (mentally, emotionally, physiologically, financially and etc.) do you need to be developed?

_____

_____

_____

_____

_____

_____

2) What pitfalls have you changed into pit stops? Explain.

_____

_____

_____

_____

3) In what areas of your attitude and leadership do you still need to be smoothed out? Explain.

_____

_____

_____

_____

_____

_____

God doesn't want to just have you. He wants to use you!

Vessels of Honor

Chapter 10: Vessels must have Passion

One of the most important things that a person must have to be a Vessel of Honor is passion. Passion is the fuel that drives you to do what it is that you have been called to do. Passion is the compass that is used to direct your life into the area that God has called and created you to be in. Passion is what keeps you focused. Passion is what keeps you energized. Passion is what refuels you when you are completely exhausted and worn out. Passion is what will get you out of bed in the early morning hours before the sun begins its ascension into the sky and to do something that no one else will do.

There is a great difference between what you can do, and what you are passionate about doing. The common denominator between the two is one word: Aptitude. Aptitude is the natural ability to do something. For instance, most human beings have the aptitude to walk upright, to hear, to smell and to touch. Aptitude is possible based on having senses. Becoming an author, playing an instrument, becoming an athlete, etc., primarily derives from aptitude. Capability + nature + potential = aptitude.

While aptitude is an important part in the process, the coupling factor to aptitude is attitude. The way you think about what you can and cannot accomplish and what you become or do, will affect your aptitude. Don't try to accomplish something simply because you see someone else doing something that looks to be fun, easy or money-making; it may not have anything to do with your particular destiny. Your aptitude affects your destiny. Your destiny is God's intended purpose for your life; not what you want it to be. It is possible to become a successful failure. A successful failure is someone who succeeds at something they were never called to do. Don't let that be you!

Just because you may have the skill, the dexterity, the platform and even the gift to do something, doesn't necessarily mean that you have the passion for it. Dexterity is a matter of skill. Passion is a matter of the heart. Vessels of Honor will always flourish in the arenas of their aptitudes, passions and abilities that are pulling or directing them. Aptitude, passions, and abilities will lead you into your element. Your element is the place where your passions and skills flourish. It's a place of complete freedom and comfort where one feels a sense of impact, purpose and destiny.

When a person is out of their element, they become a fish out of water. Typically, a fish can survive anywhere between 10 minutes to 24 hours out of their element. Although other elements are great and appear to be wonderful, the fish will only survive in the element for which it has been purposed. All fish get oxygen from water and some can absorb oxygen from the atmosphere they inhabit. Although they can absorb oxygen out of their element, their survival is totally dependent on them remaining in the environment made conducive to and for them. If the fish is out of its element longer than expected, it will die.

When we are in our element, as it is with the fish, so it is with you and me. There is an element that God has purposed for our passions, dexterities, talents, callings and gifts to flourish. When we are in our element, our passion, along with God's anointing, empower us to become what He destined and created us to be. When we are out of our element we become like that fish. We die. We don't die a death that places us into a cemetery. No, we face something far worse! This death kills our dreams, goals, visions and purpose. We die full of potential when we were purposed to die empty.

The fish out of water analogy is what is happening to many individuals who have a sense of passion, but haven't found their element of life in which to function and flow. One of the most frustrating things to face is discovering your passions, but not your element. Remember a fish can survive out of their element for a period of time. For us, what that means is we could go to college, get a degree, land a great job making a lot of money, and even become an expert in our area—but that's not our element. We could be leading an organization that is not our element. When we are out of our element, we will become frustrated after a period of time. Why? Our passions can't flourish in just any element. They only flourish when they are in the right element. No matter how good you are at something; if you are not in your element, you will not be successful or satisfied. You can be good at doing everything, but you will only be great when you are in your element.

There is an element that your gifts, callings and talents are created for and will flourish. Your element is the place where, when you are there, you can stay for hours. Where others would wear out, you would rust out because that is your element. Your element may be speaking in front of groups of people. It may be surrounded by large amounts of paperwork searching for one dollar, so that the accounting books will be balanced. It may be going into schools teaching and mentoring kids. It may be putting on a uniform, going out and serving your

Vessels of Honor

community. It may be volunteering with an organization that helps the homeless, less fortunate or those who may be going through a rough time. Your element could be going into chaotic situations and helping bring peace. It could be cooking, working with technology or animals, art, being an administrator or being in leadership.

Finding your element is more than doing things that you can do or even things that you are good at. Finding your element is finding the place that you love. Finding your element is important as it relates to understanding who you are, what you're capable of and who you are destined to be. Your personal, social, economic, financial and emotional peace will be found when you get into your element! Everyone has an element. Some have lived long lives, had families, made millions of dollars, lived in mansions and driven the best cars, but they still have not found their element.

Recently, I took a trip to Memphis, Tennessee. While I was there, I stopped in to check out the Bass Pro Shop inside of the Pyramid Center. To my surprise, there was a crocodile lying behind glass. It looked like it had to be about 12 feet long. It was huge! It was laying on a rock, simply gazing at patrons walking by it. Although the crocodile had rocks, water, and was in a setting of a make-believe forest, I wondered how this crocodile had become accustomed to an element that it was not intended for. It was given all the accoutrements of the element that it was intended for but it wasn't real. Have you become accustomed to having the accoutrements of your element while not really being in it? Have you become complacent in an environment, relationship, organization, career, role or arena that you know is not your element? If so, this is the time for you to change. You can be good anywhere, but you will not become great until you get into your element!

I heard a story about two young fish swimming down a river. On their journey, they came upon an older fish who was swimming toward them. As they passed by, the older fish said to them, "Good Morning Fellas. How's the water treating you this morning?" They smiled at the older fish and continued on their journey. Further down the river one of the young fish looked over at the other and said, "Hey, what's water?" The point of the story was that the young fish asking the question took for granted his element. He didn't realize that he was already in it. That is what being in your element will feel like. When you are there, it will be natural and adaptable to you.

Raashid K. Brown

Let me be the first to tell you, it may take time to find your element. In fact, finding your element is a journey that has a road unto itself. The road to finding your element starts internally and ends externally. It requires self-awareness and honesty to yourself. It requires commitment and focus. One of the biggest challenges that this generation has to face is distractions. Now; more than ever, there are so many distractions fighting for our attention. If you are not careful, you will spend minutes, days, months, years and decades not even in your element. The longer you stay out of your element, the more risk there is of you suffocating due to being out of "water."

Let me share with you how I found my element. I was introduced to my element, unbeknownst to me at the time, when I was in high school. I had been working steady jobs for about a

Vessels of Honor

year and one of my teachers asked me talk to peers in my life-skills class about interviewing for a job. I will admit I was nervous about it. Once I got up though, I felt at ease. My nervousness left. I was talking about things that I hadn't written down. I put my all into it; and before I knew it, I was flowing in a way that I never had before. It was in that moment that I realized communication and serving were my elements.

The first job I had was working at an amusement park. I was fourteen years old, working at a funnel cake shop. Although this atmosphere was totally new for me, I noticed that I liked serving others. As the years went by, I kept being drawn to jobs in the park that put me around people and allowed me to serve. One of the jobs I took was entitled Park Services Ambassador. The name sounds pretty, but the work was really being a janitor. Others thought the job was disgusting, but I loved it. I didn't see what they saw. They saw this as a terrible job. I saw it as serving others and being able to move around. I saw it as; when others made a mess, they called me to clean it up. Sure! It was hard work and hot days, but I really liked my job. After a few years, I was asked to become a Park Ranger.

The Park Rangers were the security officers at the amusement part. I hadn't thought about doing that type of work ever before. What got my attention about the job was, that it was a different way to serve. Once I got in the element of security work, I loved it! There would be times that I would volunteer to stay late. I wouldn't want to leave, and I couldn't wait to come in. I was promoted to a leadership position in the element and fell in love with it. One day, I got a phone call from someone I respected who asked if I'd be interested in becoming a law enforcement officer. I knew my elements (serving and communication), but I was fearful about going to another level in my element. Shortly thereafter; however, I agreed and nine years later I'm still in my element.

Great opportunities did not find me until I was in my element. Once they did find me, every level led to the next. Was it easy? Of course not. Did I make mistakes? All the time. Did I get stressed out? Yes. Did I ever get so frustrated that I wanted to quit and not look back? More times than you would imagine. What kept me focused was, I found my element and despite the many situations that arouse, I kept returning to the place where my passion flourished. My element put me in the right place for my purpose to become realized. Vessels of Honor are those who can function to their highest and best use; for God's glory, in the element for which they have been destined. Get in your water!

Vessels of Honor

Chapter Appraisal

1) What are you passionate about? What do you love to do? What would you do for fee just because it's your passion?

_____

_____

_____

_____

_____

2) What are your personal aptitudes and abilities?

_____

_____

_____

_____

3) Have you found your element? If so, what and where is it?

In order to be a Vessel of Honor, you must discover your passions and they must be in the right element.

Vessels of Honor

Chapter 11: Vessels must be Purged

Of all things that a vessel must be, I believe this last one is where most of us experience the most opposition. A vessel can have everything else done; perfected and right. But if they fail to be purged, they will not be used to His highest and best use. Being purged is something that we all must do.

The second part of the scriptural landmark of this book, and the conclusion to the thought Paul was having about Vessels of Honor and dishonor in a great house is 2 Timothy 2:21: "If a man therefore purge himself from these, he shall be a vessel unto honor, sanctified, and meet for the master's use and prepared unto every good work."

Notice who does the purge in the text. The man. The individual. Not God. There comes a point where Christians have to understand that Jesus Christ came in the form of a person and completed the work and plan of God. Once we accept Him as Lord and Savior in our lives, we have to do our part to maintain the relationship. Our relationship with Christ is not one-sided. Imagine if you were in a relationship that was one-sided. You gave all, did all and became all while the other person just received but did not give. How would you feel? Taken for granted? Not appreciated? Empty? How you would feel is exactly how God feels when we take everything that He offers without giving Him back anything.

When we see the 'purge,' we may think it means to just clean out. When Paul wrote this text he used a Greek word *ekkathairo* which literally means "completely and thoroughly clean out." Paul uses the same word in 1 Corinthians 5:7 when he says, "Purge out therefore the old leaven, that ye may be a new lump, as ye are unleavened. For even

Vessels of Honor

Christ our Passover is sacrificed for us." The word leaven is mentioned 39 times in the Bible. Each time the word is used, it is as a shadow or type of corruption or sin.

When Paul writes 'purge' he is not saying simply to clean out. He is saying to get completely, totally and entirely rid of the something. Don't just clean it out, but thoroughly clean it out. If someone said they had washed a dish but you can still see food stains on the dish, it would be safe to say that the person had cleaned the dish but had not thoroughly cleaned it. To be thoroughly and entirely clean, one must make sure there is no left-over residue of what was before.

If there is still residue in your life of what you used to be and what you used to do, then you have to become the dish that claims to be clean but still has noticeable stains. You have not been purged. You cannot be who you were and who you are at the same time. You cannot be a Vessel of Honor who is purged and a vessel of dishonor at the same time. In the moment that God wants to use you, He needs you to be clean, available, empty and ready to be used. He has done the work of sanctification (setting you apart), and now is the time that you must do your part to ensure that you are set apart. Purge!

In order to thoroughly and entirely clean out your life, there are some things you are going to have to stop doing. Seek deliverance from strongholds that you have been dealing with. Those struggles, addictions, practices and secret sins are preventing you from being used. God wants you to be clean. In fact, He died in your place because He knew that you could not clean yourself. You and I owed a serious debt, and we didn't have a means to pay for the debt that we owed. The debt we owed was the debt of sin. We needed something to clean us from the guilt and stains of sin. Christ paid a debt that He didn't owe. Even when He became a man, He still didn't owe the debt like we did. Romans 5:8 says, "But God demonstrates His own love toward us, in that while we were yet sinners, Christ did for us." His death was a business transaction that paid for our sins.

So now that He paid for our sins, it's up to us to ensure that we are available for Him to use. There's nothing worse than paying for something that you can't use because it is not functional, or not working properly. It's an inconvenience! One has to make adjustments or go back and exchange the malfunctioning one for one that works. Christ does not trade us back in when we are not working properly, although He has every right to do so. He exhibits patience and allows us to get ourselves together. He puts us in environments and atmospheres that challenge us to become better. He allows us to come across a book or hear a message or causes us to pause on a television station, so we can hear someone telling us to get our lives together.

God does not play favorites. He doesn't have certain vessels that He uses, because they are His favorite choice. In fact, the vessels who always seem to be used are the ones who have purged themselves from sin and have placed themselves in a position to be used of God anywhere and at any time. When we fully understand that, I believe there will be no need for jealousy of other people. Why be jealous that someone else is used by God to do great things? You can do the same if you purge

Vessels of Honor

yourself and remain in a position where God can use you anywhere at any time.

Vessel, you need to purge! What you are in need of is available for you to have, but you may not be available to receive it. There is sin hidden somewhere in your camp. While Joshua was journeying to his destiny with the children of Israel after the death of Moses, his champion victories came to an abrupt stop once someone committed a secret sin. Joshua chapter 7 records the secret sin of Achan. In Chapter 6, the children of Israel won the battle against Jericho and were instructed not to take anything from the land. Achan took something and hid the item in his tent. He covered it up. No one knew he had it…except God. God judged the whole nation, causing 36 men to die and the nation of Israel to lose the battle of Ai. Ai was a small city. In fact the report of the spies was to not even send the whole army. Three thousand men were sent to fight the battle; which they should have overwhelmingly won, but because of one man's sin, the whole nation lost.

There's a possibility that this could be a season of overwhelming victory and wins in your life, but you are losing simply because of who you are or what you are attached to. There may be certain people, places or things causing you not to become who you are intended to be. You may be guilty by association. Vessels of Honor usually aren't housed in the same cabinet as vessels of dishonor. A paper cup isn't placed in the china cabinet with the china. They don't belong together. They are suitable based upon their need, but together they disagree. Don't become complacent with paper cups when you are fine china.

Vessels of Honor

Defeat does not just happen. When you start to lose in an area, know that there is a reason why. Most people stop once they start losing, without figuring out why. Was it the right season/time? Did you prepare hard enough for it? Did you make the right decisions? Was there something that you could have done better? Did you seek God to ensure that you were moving in the right manner? Everything matters. Defeat often serves as an indicator that something was misaligned or out of step. Joshua lost this battle, because someone in the camp was out of alignment with the will of God. The story records that before Joshua lost the battle, he did something immediately. He sought the Lord.

A true sign of your maturity in your walk with God, is how fast you are willing to seek His face during adversity. Joshua didn't wait a week. He immediately sought God as to the reason why he lost the battle. You and I must do the same! We must seek God when defeat happens, realizing that defeat doesn't just happen. Joshua not only lost the battle, he lost soldiers—36 to be exact. There were casualties of this war. Joshua had not lost a battle up until this point. Every battle before this one was a win.

After Joshua turned to God and sought Him as to why he lost, he got a response. God told Joshua to get up, and then He told Joshua why he lost the battle. "Israel has sinned" (verse 11). Wait! In actuality; we know that only one person had sinned, but God said the whole nation had sinned. This again shows that God judged them all for the sake of one. God says, in verse 12, that Israel; the nation, could not stand before its enemies because the sin in them made them liable to destruction. Did you hear that? Their association with one man in the camp made the whole nation liable to destruction. Are you connected with, mingling with or associated with people who make you liable to destruction?

God was not looking for excuses, not for sociological assessment of what caused the defeat. God was looking to get things back in order and alignment. God tells Joshua to sanctify the people. God never moves in unclean vessels. If Israel was to be used of God, the nation had to purge the sin from out of itself. The method to determine the sinner was ingenious. The next morning, all Israel was assembled by tribe, by family, by household and man by man. Achan was then located.

In verses 20-21, Achan gives his explanation regarding what he took and why. Achan heard the rule not to take anything in Jericho, but he did so anyway and thus caused the whole camp to be judged. Upon hearing Achan's story, Joshua sent messengers to Achan's tent and removed all the accursed spoils. Due to sin, Achan and his family were killed. He and his family were purged from them. Had Achan and his family not been killed, Israel would have lost every battle and would have been overtaken by their enemies.

As a vessel of honor, you must find the Achan that is in you. Achan may not be a person, it may be a habit. It may be an addiction. It may be cheating, lying, stealing or gossip. What is your Achan? Whatever your Achan is, you need to find it and purge it. Kill it! Do you know why it was essential that the whole family of Achan was killed? So that there would not be a chance that someone from his bloodline would rise up and commit the same offense that would cause defeat for the nation again. For the nation to purge itself, it had to kill

Vessels of Honor

everything and anything that was connected to it. Joshua 7:28 says that the whole nation played a part in getting rid of Achan, his family, his animals and his tent. Emotions were not a concern. Whatever caused defeat had to be purged from the nation. After Achan was destroyed, God gave Joshua a strategy that caused him to win the next time around.

There are some defeats that will turn into victories once you have fully purged Achan out of the camp. A vessel that has leaven, corruption or sin in it is one that will not experience victory. No matter how much you pray or make plans; if there is sin in your life, you will not become a Vessel of Honor. Vessels of Honor are the only vessels suitable for the Master to use consistently The Master only uses those who are suitable. The goal is to become suitable. Christ died and paid your debt so that you; in turn, could become suitable to His highest and best use. Suitable vessels are ones that God can use anywhere and at anytime.

Become a Vessel of Honor…God wants to use you!

Vessels of Honor

Chapter Appraisal

1) What hidden things, addictions, habits and practices do you need to purge?

_____

_____

_____

_____

_____

_____

2) In what areas are you experiencing defeat due to failing to purge?

_____

_____

_____

_____

3) What persons, places or things do you need to disconnect from in order to become a Vessel of Honor?

Vessels of Honor

A personal letter to you!

Thank you for reading *Vessels of Honor*. This book came about during some seasons of my life where I had to confront who I really was. As I have stated, there is a certain type of vessel that God is looking for, and He will only use this particular vessel to accomplish His will.

It is my personal belief that before you can become a Vessel of Honor, you must discover and develop a relationship with Christ. I believe church has become great at drawing people, but may have dropped the ball as it relates to discipleship. We can't make disciples without discipleship. Discipleship is essentially becoming disciplined in our walk with God. It is not enough to accept Christ into our lives without some responsibility to make this world better by letting Him use us for His will and His glory. He saved us so that we may serve one another. Everyday you should be having some interaction with what I like to call "The Three C's"—Christ, Church, and Community!

If you have already accepted Christ into your life, I want to encourage you to become a better disciple. We all could be better. Live your life in a way that is completely submitted to God, so that He can use you anywhere at anytime. Stay focused and stay committed.

If you have not accepted Jesus Christ into your life, I'd like to extend to you the greatest invitation which is the opportunity to accept Jesus Christ into your life. He died for you and wants to give you eternal life. He wants you to become a part of His family. He wants to use you in ways you can't even imagine!

If you want to accept Jesus Christ, pray this prayer with me:

Vessels of Honor

Heavenly Father, I come to You confessing that I'm a sinner in need of Your grace. Forgive me Lord for my sins. I acknowledge that you; Jesus, came to Earth, died for my sins, and You were raised from the dead. Come into my heart. I want You as my Lord and Savior. In Jesus name, Amen!

Now that you have accepted Christ into your life, find a Bible believing and teaching church where you can begin to grow and become equipped to become a Vessel of Honor. God has GREAT things in store for you. Be Great!!

www.ingramcontent.com/pod-product-compliance
Lightning Source LLC
Chambersburg PA
CBHW071201160426
43196CB00011B/2154